Winning Your Players through Trust, Loyalty, and Respect

A Soccer Coach's Guide

DeAngelo Wiser

D1607619

Oakamoor
Publishing

An imprint of Bennion Kearny Ltd.

Published in 2016 by Oakamoor Publishing, an imprint of Bennion Kearny Limited.

ISBN: 978-1-910773-30-7

Published by Oakamoor Publishing, Bennion Kearny Limited
6 Woodside
Churnet View Road
Oakamoor
Staffordshire
ST10 3AE

www.BennionKearny.com

So many challenges had to be dealt with to reach this point. It took time, patience, and perseverance. The inspiration and guiding light in my life is my wife Nancy. I dedicate this book to her for all she's given up for me.

Acknowledgements

I want to thank my players whose determination and sacrifices make our game great. It was a joy to be on the sideline and witness every effort to succeed night in and night out. Players win games, coaches win strategy, and many lessons are learned by both along the way. They taught me so much about enjoying the journey, laughter, and toughness, and I will always be grateful.

The many parents who spent hours assisting us in every way possible were the backbone of our program, and they did a splendid job of supporting their children's efforts and allowing our program to shine. Their patience and understanding was appreciated.

To all the officials I met along the way, I can only say no one appreciates you more for what you give the game than me. I truly enjoyed our conversations and getting to know you.

Being an assistant coach takes special traits that can't be explained. The assistant coaches I worked with were the best. I appreciate everything they did to benefit the players. Without them, we would not have been as successful and so many positive moments would have been lost. Their friendship and dedication is something I will never forget.

There were many colleagues who shaped my style and ability to handle challenges early in my career. Pat Neilsen, Jim Scobee, Frank Conyers, Joe Crouse, Jay Buffin, Steve Showen and Steve Sandberg all had a positive impact on my career. Each was unique, but all stressed that the athlete's wellbeing comes first. They all believed in me and gave me the opportunity to teach and coach. Truly a debt I will never be able to repay.

My involvement in the National Soccer Coaches Association of America (NSCAA) had a profound impact on my career. During a 20-year span, I attended every convention and earned diplomas at residential courses, learning from the best clinicians in the world. There is no other association so dedicated to its members.

I want to express my sincere gratitude to James Lumsden-Cook and Bennion Kearny Publishing for their tireless efforts in allowing me the opportunity to share this book with players and coaches.

Testimonials

"Teamwork and Character"

I have worked with hundreds of coaches over the years, and there is no doubt that Coach DeAngelo Wiser is in a very elite class of coaches who understand the true value of sport. Coach Wiser's teams are not only well-coached in the sport of soccer, but his athletes are also highly motivated because they know that he genuinely cares about them as people.

Using a people-building methodology, Coach Wiser teaches his teams all of the important values inherent in sport – teamwork, character, discipline, and positivity – just to name a few. From my observations, a Coach Wiser team always had great team dynamics and content players, regardless of wins and losses.

In short, Coach Wiser invests in and mentors his players and is a winner through and through.

Jason Neidell | Head Womens Soccer Coach | Western Kentucky University

"Leader and Role Model"

As superintendent of Jessamine County Schools for nine years, I had the privilege of working with hundreds of coaches - most of whom were exceptional men and women who loved their athletes and their sport. DeAngelo Wiser stands out among that elite group as a leader and a standard-bearer. The words that come to mind when I think of Coach Wiser are humble, kind, and devoted. He is a man of character known for his integrity and commitment to his athletes above self and status. He was a celebrated coach, but, more importantly, he was a role model for his players, their families, and his colleagues.

Lu Young | University of Kentucky College of Education Faculty Member | Former Superintendent | Jessamine County Schools

"The legacy you leave"

I've been involved in athletics for 27 years and have never been around someone that truly understood athletics and life in a way that Coach Wiser has shown me. One of the greatest gifts as a coach is to know that your players leave your program better people. Getting the chance as an athletic director to work with him and getting to know him on a personal level, he has changed the way I look at life and how I approach athletics. One of my favorite quotes is "Let someone else praise you and not your own mouth, a stranger, and not your own lips." Coach Wiser is one of the most humble coaches and would go out of his way to make sure you received recognition over him. He is one of a kind and in my eyes he is our John Wooden.

Daniel Sandlin | Athletic Director | East Jessamine High & Middle Schools

"The right decision"

I was blessed to work with Coach Wiser for seven years in a classroom setting. He always had a plan and could see the big picture at all times. His coaching wisdom, ability to motivate people, calm demeanor, and thoughtfulness were displayed every day. His common message was the right decision is not always easy and the easy decision is not always right. I am a much better coach, person, and teacher for having spent part of my career with him. I am forever grateful for our time together.

Mike Bowlin | Head Football Coach | East Jessamine High School

"A classroom on grass"

Coach Wiser's commitment and passion for his players to excel not only on the field but also in the classroom was evident from my first conversation with him. Coach Wiser is truly a "players' coach." His knowledge of the game and manner in which he coaches is truly a classroom on grass. There is constant reinforcement and enthusiasm challenging each player to improve daily. DeAngelo Wiser is a role model for those who aspire to be a head coach in any sport.

Ken Cox | District Athletic Director | Jessamine County Schools

Table of Contents

Introduction

Dreams can never escape us unless we give them permission.

When we're hired as a coach, we tend to think about the white collar aspects of coaching, such as championships, award banquets, developing All-Americans, personal recognition and much more. It's only natural to have dreams of success, but the reality is that challenges must be dealt with on our way to that dream. That's when we need that blue collar, lunch pail, hard hat, roll your sleeves up, and grind it out attitude to carry us forwards. Knowing the best way to navigate and deal with challenges – and in my career I have faced many – is the key to how effective we'll be with our teams. They always made me stronger, strengthened my character, and let me know that I had the greatest job in the world. Where else could you have a mobile classroom with the opportunity to positively impact so many young people? It's not surprising that my first challenge was breaking into the profession, but I was so fortunate to have inspiration from the love of my life. I could not have made it without my beautiful wife, Nancy.

My story is not one of overcoming insurmountable odds or adversity, just simply persevering and never giving up on a dream. Between my Junior and Senior year in college I joined the United States Marine Corps in hopes of becoming an officer. During Officer Candidate School at Quantico, I trained with the best and learned leadership skills that would serve me well. However, after graduating from OCS I learned that I required more college coursework to graduate on time. That would mean returning to OCS which wasn't a decision I wanted to make. My career in the military was not to be.

After graduating from college with a degree in Physical Education, I was unable to secure a teaching or coaching position. My field was crowded, and I had no understanding of what it took to compete for a job and no connections to assist me in any way. So I began working in a factory and got married. My young career would see me working for an industrial furnace startup company traveling the North American Continent. I also ended up selling cars and managing major automobile dealerships. This detour from my dream would last 14 years and take me into my late 30's, but I still longed for the chance to teach and help young people, even though my teaching certificate had expired.

The motivation and determination to pursue my dream came in the form of a check for $0.00 for a month's work which bore no results. Can you imagine what that would feel like? Right then and there my wife and I decided we could survive on her salary while I went back to college for a Masters' degree needed for certification. Little did we know it would take us four years and many tasks (I mowed a lot of yards!) to finally reach that dream. So at 40 years of age, feeling as excited as ever, I finally fulfilled my life's ambition of teaching and helping young people become responsible adults, along with coaching soccer.

However, my first teaching job was not what I had planned. Through my loyalty to substitute teaching for one particular school system, I was asked to teach full time at an alternative school. This turned out to be a perfect fit for me and my new students. I had the same 15 students all day, all on independent study courses and all with various challenges to overcome in order to succeed. I really felt I made a difference in their lives through encouragement, caring, and teaching them life skills which – at the time – they needed more than Science, English, and Math. Ultimately they were my first team and taught me so much. It would be four years before I'd land my first physical education job, but I'll always cherish my time at the alternative school, and the influence these young people, teachers, and administrators had on my life.

When I was first asked to coach the girls' soccer program, which had only been in existence for one year, I agreed although it was not the sport in which I had the most experience. So I set about reviewing and revisiting the game as quickly as possible, reading and viewing everything current I could find, becoming nationally certified, attending clinics and residential courses, and watching the sport at every level.

Now 357 games, and a countless number of outstanding young athletes, assistant coaches, and athletic directors, later, I feel very blessed. The influence my players and their parents had on me helped validate and strengthen my character and values. Because of them, my fellow coaches, administrators, and officials, I've enjoyed and relished my coaching experience. It would have been easy to give up on my dream, but with the help of my wife, I was able to make that dream a reality.

Dreams cause us to hope, and inspire us to do things which seem impossible. Never give up on your dreams. They not only affect you but so many others as well. I wish you the best in your career.

Coach DeAngelo Wiser

Section 1
Trust, Loyalty, and Respect

"The absolute heart of loyalty is to value those people who tell you the truth, not just those people who tell you what you want to hear. In fact, you should value them most. Because they have paid you the compliment of leveling with you and assuming you can handle it." Pat Summitt

Trust, Loyalty, and Respect are three old-school terms that shine as brightly today as they did in years gone by. They are virtually forgotten in today's coaching lingo, buried under a sea of technology and social media, but as relevant and needed as any words we use.

Have you ever considered what allows you to reach your players with conviction? It's the Trust, Loyalty, and Respect you've earned through the tough decisions you make every day with your team. Our communication with our players, and even those who don't make our team, has a huge impact on their lives. It's that communication which matches our actions when accountability is necessary; it's that communication which gives us credibility.

When moments arise outside the game for our players such as illness, death and tragedy, our ability and willingness to drop everything and comfort our players is paramount. When they have questions about their roles on the team, and we give them honest answers, we earn Trust, Loyalty, and Respect. Knowing what's really important and putting players' well-being first is a key element of coaching.

In this unit, we embrace the key elements for reaching our players.

- Are you able to trust your players in key situations?
- Do you feel the need to orchestrate every movement?
- Can you sense the moment something isn't right with your team?
- Have you shared with your players the responsibility of representing their school outside the game?
- Do you take the time to meet with every player concerning their role on the team?

1

Winning Your Players

Coaches spend hours searching for the perfect activity, book, or DVD to motivate, inspire and engage players throughout the year. If you've coached for any period of time, just look around. Your office is probably littered with books, DVDs and other materials used only once and then filed away.

Through these various resources, we seek special words and phrases to use at just the right time, like tournament time, to perform magic with our team. It often gives us comfort to find a theme that agrees with our philosophy at a particular moment. Perhaps the thoughts or writing of others give us credibility with our team? Maybe they give us the confidence to ask more from our team than we ever have? Maybe they help us to convince our players that they are greater than they think?

Everything you use comes back to you. It's you – the coach – that your players are listening to. It's you – the coach – your players see. But what is it that ultimately opens the door, allowing you to reach your players and give your words meaning?

Trust, Loyalty, and Respect.

Trust, Loyalty, and Respect aren't bought in a store or online. They are earned. And there is one key that unlocks your ability to earn Trust, Loyalty, and Respect with your team… it's *how you make and communicate decisions*.

As the following illustration makes clear, we are faced with decisions every day. Some are challenges that come from conflict, confrontation, controversy, and choices; others originate from winning, success, awards, losing, media, and championships.

Throughout the year, in every situation requiring a decision, your team is watching, learning and storing away examples of your character and integrity. Do your actions match your words? When a decision isn't based on expectations set by you and your players, and inconsistent, you lose some degree of Trust, Loyalty, and Respect. If this pattern continues over a period of time (across different situations), you stand the chance of losing your team altogether. Sure, they'll listen to what you say, and probably go through the motions, but your words will have no meaning.

However, as coaches, if we're consistent with our decisions, even in tough times, and they are based on expectations established at the beginning of the year, our ability to earn Trust, Loyalty, and Respect is enhanced.

It's at the *moment* of making a decision, based on strong character and integrity, that we win or lose our team. It doesn't mean they will like it, but they understand expectations must be followed. Simply stated, when we win over our players, when they trust our leadership and we earn their loyalty, it frees them up mentally to play with passion, enthusiasm, and optimism.

After all, isn't that what we all want?!?

2

Making Every Player Feel Important

Many of us were fortunate to have played on teams where we felt a special part of a group of outstanding athletes. There were probably teammates we associated with, or whom we liked, more than others but the environment created by our coach made us all feel important regardless of whether we were the star player, coming off the bench, or rarely playing. How is that possible?

Think about your family. There could be anywhere from one to 10 children with one or two parents or stepparents. Your parents or guardians did their best to make you all feel important, and at times that would have been a huge undertaking.

Now that we're coaching, how can we do our best to make the experience wonderful for 15 to 35 players? Can it be done? Should it be a priority? I believe it should.

With all the responsibilities of planning practice, game strategy, paperwork and much more, it's not easy to focus on this aspect of coaching. For most of us, we just need a refresher on what we can do to maximize the results for each player, and make them feel a special part of our team.

1. **GREET** - Speak and make eye contact with every player, every day. It sets the tone for practice and the game. They have to know you're glad to see them, and you're looking forward to seeing them in the game or practice.

2. **ROLE** - If you keep a player, you have an idea of how they can help the team. Let them know their role as you see it at the beginning of the season, and ask them how they see themselves contributing to the team.

3. **COMMUNICATE** - We all communicate with our players about the game, but just asking about their school work, their

club team or their family shows genuine interest in their welfare.

4. **CHALLENGE** - Each player should be challenged during practice and the game with urgency and intensity, whether they're the best player or not. Never give up on a player. If they're not performing or improving, talk about them with your assistants and develop a plan.

5. **EVALUATE** - Find the time, either through your efforts or your assistants, to evaluate each player's progress at intervals throughout the season. They need guidance in ways to improve their skill and mental approach to the game.

6. **INCLUDE** - Find a way to include players in decisions that impact the team. Players don't want to be left out and often become disgruntled when they are. That inclusion could expose leadership skills not yet revealed.

7. **LISTEN** - If a player has an issue or idea, take the time to listen. It may (or may not) have merit, but either way, it's important to them. Clear your mind and any task you may be working on and show – through your body language – that you're tuned in. Never be too busy to listen. We often learn so much from our players.

8. **OPPORTUNITY** - Give players the opportunity to shine in game or practice situations. You kept them for a reason, let them play. If you don't, at least tell them why. Do your best to find the right situations.

9. **CONTRIBUTE** - Let players know how they contribute to your team's success. Every player wants to feel they contribute something to the team. It may just be a wonderful attitude and willingness to help their teammates that make them special. If so, let them know. Every player has positive attributes that your team needs. Highlight them at every opportunity.

10. **CONGRATULATE** - When a player does something special, whether giving 150% in practice or providing a great pass during a game, let them know how proud you are. Take the time to ask them, "How did that make *you* feel?"

The pressure we put on ourselves to guide our team throughout the year often gets in the way of truly working to fulfill our players' needs to feel important. Every player needs to hear you say or do something that keeps them coming back and giving a monumental effort to help their teammates. It doesn't take a lot of time, and the opportunity is there every day. Take the time, today, to make your players feel special, and let them know how grateful you are for all they bring to the team. It will do far more than winning a game.

3

The Game Outside
The Lines

During the season you'll have the opportunity to take on the most important opponent you'll ever play. Being successful is a must. And yet, this opponent is not even on your match schedule!

We've coined this contest the "Stumbles". It's the time(s) when our players make a misstep (usually out of character) and require a reset.

It shows up when one of them is involved in a situation such as failing a class, getting in a fight, putting up an irresponsible social media post, missing practice, missing the bus, or other conduct that's not acceptable, That's when you have to hold them accountable. The key is to make sure they understand what is expected of them early on, and what will happen if they fall short.

Players expect to be held accountable, and when we – as coaches – do anything less it costs us in Trust, Loyalty, and Respect. In essence, it's the point where we win or lose that player, and ultimately our team.

These situations often happen around a big match, at tournament time, or before a championship game. The end result may require a player to sit out that game which can complicate thought processes, but it should never cloud your judgment regarding accountability.

If you've coached for any period of time, you've probably observed coaches who, with seemingly good intentions, try to help their players by lessening or avoiding any punishment so they can play. After all, they say, "Why should the team suffer?" They have a point, but players have to learn that everything they do within a team setting has an impact on others.

Let's look at factors that may harm your credibility:

- **IS IT ONE OF MY BEST PLAYERS?** While it's natural to hope a key player isn't involved in unacceptable conduct, it really should have no bearing on their accountability. It doesn't matter which player it is; they have to answer for their actions.

- **WHAT GAME IS NEXT?** Checking your schedule to see who you play next is okay. But not if you find out it's a rival, conference, or district game, and your immediate thought is to find a way to get a particular player eligible at any cost.

- **CAN I DELAY THE PUNISHMENT BY SKIPPING A GAME, OR WAIT UNTIL NEXT SEASON**? Trying to justify skipping a game before the punishment kills your credibility with the team. Understand the team sees what you're doing, and, if you don't do it the same way for every player, you've lost them completely.

- **I'LL LET THE TEAM VOTE.** Letting the team vote is really bailing out on making the decision. We all know the team will usually vote to let a player play, and pay for their actions later. Make the decision and do the right thing because you're their leader.

- **CAN I COME UP WITH SOME SIMPLE, IMMEDIATE PUNISHMENT?** Telling the teacher, AD, or Administrator, that you'll run and run the offending player in practice after the big game is not the right message to send to your colleagues. Take the game away from the player and the lesson will be learned, not only by that player but the whole team.

- **IF THEY APOLOGIZE, IS THAT GOOD ENOUGH?** Players should naturally apologize. It won't pay the bill for their actions, but it carries a lot of weight by defining their character. Apologies should be expected.

- **I'LL TALK TO THE TEACHER.** If you want to visit a teacher to make sure you have all the facts concerning something like a low grade, I believe that's okay. I am against asking the teacher – at that point – what the player can do to make up the grade so they can play tomorrow. It sends the wrong message. The player had a lot of time to work on their grade and decided not to. If you let them off the hook, you'll be begging again. Is that helping your player?

Let's look at questions we need to ask:

- **WHO IS IT?** We just need to know what player or players are involved. The impact may be more far-reaching than any game we play. Remember, it's someone on *your* team, and you have a responsibility to talk with them as soon as possible.

- **WHAT ARE THE FACTS? AM I SATISFIED WE HAVE ALL THE NECESSARY INFORMATION?** Gather any and all information concerning the incident from as many people as possible. You need a clear picture of what went on. Make sure you have all the facts before making a decision.

- **DO THEY NEED TO SIT IT OUT WHILE WE INVESTIGATE?** If there is any doubt about eligibility, ask your AD for advice. Jeopardizing your season is not something to take lightly. Sitting out one game pales into insignificance in comparison to forfeiting a season.

- **SHOULD THE ATHLETIC DIRECTOR OR ADMINISTRATOR BE INVOLVED?** Include your AD or Administrator in all incidents. They should never hear about it from a parent or someone outside your school system. From a legal standpoint, it's a safeguard for you.

- **WHAT IS THE ACCOUNTABILITY?** Make sure you have the right punishment for any given situation. The players understood this at the beginning of the season when they established ground rules with you.

- **DO THE PARENTS KNOW?** Contact the parents early on, and let them know the situation. Face-to-face communication is best. When you've completed the process, let them know what has to take place. Make sure they hear it from you and not from their son or daughter.

- **SHOULD THE TEAM KNOW?** I would advise always consulting with your AD before holding a team meeting with respect to legal and privacy issues. You may want an Administrator to conduct the meeting with you present. The team doesn't need to hear rumors from anyone else, just the facts you can give them.

Dealing with these situations is never easy, but imagine if your team had neither expectations nor any accountability for their actions. Those expectations that you and the team worked on at the beginning of the season must stand for something and be the standard your team lives up to. When you involve the players in that process, it's not just what you believe; it's what *they* believe as well.

There is never a good time for a player to make a bad decision (stumble) that impacts his or her teammates. Lessons learned are tough on everyone, but by using all the character and integrity you have and making the best decision possible, you'll build that Trust, Loyalty, and Respect you need for the rest of the year.

It's not about making everyone happy; it's about winning a game bigger than any opponent. Opportunities present themselves throughout the season to guide our players in making quality decisions that will impact their lives. It's at that point we have to remember our priority is developing the person as much as the player.

4

Do You Trust Your Players?

Are you able to trust your players in a game situation? Do you give them opportunities to make mistakes? Do they know you trust them? Or do you feel the need to be in control of practically every situation?

I witness coaches, every day, who scream instructions continuously from the sideline during a game. For some, it's intended to be meaningful information. For others, it's a way to let go of nervous energy.

Why do they feel the need to verbally control every pass, every run, every aspect of the game? It's expected behavior in basketball games as coaches run up and down the sideline, but what about other sports in large outdoor venues? A player on the other side of the field has no chance to hear exactly what the coach is shouting.

What about on the job? How would we react if a boss was running up and down the hall screaming instructions to his or her employees every second? We'd think it was absurd. So why is it that coaches struggle, from time to time, with trusting their players? Is there a way to let our athletes make the majority of decisions during a contest? It all depends on your style of coaching.

How can a coach get on the path to building a program that enables players to make sound decisions during a game? Here are some steps to take.

Establishing a Program of Trusting Our Players:

1. **TEACH / TEACH / TEACH** - Begin in practice. In every activity, teach the decision-making aspect of solving the challenge as well as the skill. Paint a picture your players can see.

2. **COMMUNICATE** - Explain your game or match expectations and related benefits for the player and the team. Every situation on the field creates unique solutions and possibilities. Players need to know that you are allowing them to decide which solution is best.

3. **REFRAIN** - After a questionable decision, choose an appropriate time to talk with the player. Take your emotions out of the equation if it's during the heat of a game. In practice, you may want to talk right away, taking advantage of a teachable moment. During a game, it may be after you take your player out of the action, or even after the game.

4. **RELIVE** - Ask your players to revisit situations, visualizing what they experienced. Listen, Listen, Listen. Allow them to talk without feeling you have to jump in and correct every sentence, thought, or idea.

5. **OPTIONS** - Did they see other options available, or were there any? They will know what the right decision should have been 99% of the time. Tell them you have faith in their ability and know they'll get it right the next time. Showing confidence will give them the courage to make decisions.

6. **FREEDOM** - Share with players how mistakes are a natural part of the game. It's what they do after a mistake that counts the most. When you free a player's mind, it allows them to make good decisions without feeling pressure from you and lets them resume play more quickly.

7. **CATCH THEM BEING GOOD** - When they get it right, let them know! Praise, Praise, Praise. In practice, stop the activity and replay it with the same successful sequence of events and decisions.

8. **TRUST** - Let go, and allow players to make decisions and grow! It may take time if you feel the need to always be in control. At every game, give up just a little bit more, and you'll be amazed at what your players can do.

A perfect example of putting trust in a player's decision – that I will never forget – happened to me after a tough battle leading to a shoot-out.

Penalty shoot-outs are the most agonizing situation in any soccer game. At that point, two teams have battled it out for 110 minutes with no clear winner. Usually, all the players are exhausted and mentally drained, whether they admit it or not. That was the situation we faced in a regional final against our fiercest rival, several years ago, when we had to pick five players to shoot. Never an easy task, especially when your talent is evenly balanced.

In addition, this particular game would be the end of an era because the next year we would both be heading to tougher districts and regions. We had won three regional titles, and our opponent had won two, and now the chances of us meeting in a regional final again were slim. After this night, we'd both have three regional titles, or we'd have four, and they'd have two. I had a lot of faith that we'd take home number four, but in penalty kicks, anything is possible. "Coach, I need your list," the referee shouted as I thought of who best to put forward as our five shooters while discussing it with my assistant coaches.

As I mingled with our players, Erica, our captain took me aside and said, "Coach, let Megan shoot. She's great in PK's, and I know she can do it." As the idea was processed, I acknowledged her and walked away. So much to consider, and I didn't want to make a mistake.

Finally, I looked at my list, thought of how much I trusted Erica's opinion, and put Megan's name down. We would win our fourth regional title that night and Megan would make her shot. Certainly a joyous occasion for our team, and a moment of trust between a player and a coach, that I will never forget.

The benefits of allowing players to make decisions are endless. Here are seven:

1. **LEADERS -** Your team doesn't need leaders if you don't allow them to make decisions on and off the field. When you teach them to make sound decisions, you allow them to lead. Even if they, at the time, don't know the right decision, there is someone out there that does. They're your leaders, and they grow in this atmosphere.

2. **STRONGER INDIVIDUALS -** Life is about making decisions. Often there is no one there to guide you or help, and decisions have to be made. You're getting your players ready for that time.

3. **KEY MOMENTS -** With a few seconds or minutes to go, you may not be able to yell loudly enough for a player to hear what you expect. Teaching them to make decisions will allow you to relax and let the players influence the outcome when it's needed most.

4. **PLAYERS' TEAM -** Players will always have more passion and pride in a team where they feel comfortable and able to make decisions during a game. By showing confidence in their

abilities to make those decisions, you'll make them feel a part of something bigger.

5. **SUCCESS** - It is wonderful to see a player's face and reaction when they do something remarkable. Most don't realize it's thanks to finding the courage to make a great decision. By taking time in practice to teach that process (as well as before and after a game) you've put the player in a position to succeed.

6. **CONFIDENCE** - As players' confidence levels progress during their careers, they'll feel more comfortable coming to you with positive suggestions for practice and games. Ultimately you're building assistant coaches on and off the field that will benefit you and your team.

7. **REWARDING** - As a coach, we have to remember what we do is always about the players. Our responsibility is not only about what players are now, but what they can become. One of the most rewarding aspects of coaching is seeing a player after their career with you and realizing how they've progressed. Remember, you have a small part in that!

Successful teams always have players on the field who feel comfortable and confident in making challenging decisions. It doesn't happen overnight, and they'll make mistakes just as we do. As coaches, we have to provide an environment for that trust to grow and prosper.

Trusting your players is one of the greatest gifts you could ever give them. Take time in practice to share your expectations and then – when a player comes to you in a critical situation *with a solution* – you'll know you've done your job.

5

Can You Read Your Team?

Having learned my trade from several top coaches, I've noticed one trait that defines them. A trait that is often overlooked. It's their ability to READ their teams. But, what exactly does that mean?

I believe it's the ability to sense the mood, attitude, effort, performance or outlook of your team at any moment.

Do you have the ability to read your team? What gives you that sense? Most of us know we can read our team during, or before, a game with respect to their level of effort, execution, and mood present. It allows us to make adjustments. But what about in other situations such as practice, away from the field, a meeting, or at a function? Can we pick up on signals indicating a problem or issue? I believe there are skills that give great coaches the edge:

- **GREAT LISTENER** - Asking short questions allows players to speak. Listen with intent to understand and do not respond immediately. Players will tell you their concerns and worries if you allow them the opportunity and time.

- **TRUSTWORTHY** - Are you able to handle most problems? Can you handle a crisis without berating individuals in front of the team? This is critical for future trust. We want players to come to us when something is bothering them and if you've built trust, they will.

- **OBSERVER** - Being able to read body language, moods and attitudes is a must. It may tell you more than any words uttered. The key may be letting the issue play out before approaching a player or players.

- **EXPERIENCE** - Reading other players and teams previously will give you the experience you need in future situations. However, most situations are different and must be treated as such. Experience will give you a sense of whether to intervene right away or let the players work it out.

- **COMMUNICATION** - Ask more questions than offer solutions. Leading and guiding someone through a problem and letting them see the answers is much more important than simply stating your solution. You want to develop problem solvers.

- **CALM DEMEANOR/PATIENCE** - The ability to stay calm and be a leader in a firestorm is critical. It is also important for *not* making the situation bigger than it is.

- **RESPECT THE PLAYER** - While you may have seen a particular situation many times in your career, remember this may be new to the player talking to you. Don't downplay its significance or belittle the player for being upset over an issue they've never faced. Reinforce all the positive traits they bring to the team and guide them through possible solutions.

The ability to read your team, while seeming to be an easy task, can be very complicated. If you read the situation wrongly or react hastily, those involved may be reluctant to trust you in the future. Walking that fine line between intervening and letting a situation play out comes with experience, but that doesn't guarantee you'll be 100% right in every situation.

Often letting it play out may cost your team more than you expected. Here are some things to consider:

- Will this impact everyone?
- What might the outcome become if left unattended?
- What is the maturity level of the players involved?
- Have these players had issues before?
- When should I say something?
- What should I say?
- Do I know all the facts?

Letting it play out is very risky. Most situations never go away by themselves, and when you have a sense that something is wrong it's probably better to err on the side of caution by intervening early than doing nothing at all.

As a coach, you know when something isn't right, so trust your instinct enough to go ahead and get your team back on track. Your ability to read your team is paramount to their success.

6

Respect: Hard to Earn, Easy to Lose

Dictionary.com defines respect as *Esteem for or a sense of the worth or excellence of a person, a personal quality or ability.* How do you define respect? Whom do you respect? Why? How is respect earned?

We sometimes seem to respect those we've never met. What traits do we see? Is it the way they carry themselves, the fact that they're successful, how they come across in an interview, seeing how they react under pressure?

I believe there are five key areas where respect can be earned as a coach/leader. It is, without a doubt, the #1 attribute you must have to be effective. Without it, your team or organization just comes to work and does its job. If you have it, the team comes to work eager and passionate to accomplish new and exciting things with a willing attitude. Every day, as leaders, we have to realize that respect can vanish in an instant due to our actions or words.

Here are my must-haves to earn respect:

- **WALK THE WALK** - If you expect more from your team, expect more from yourself. Be a shining example by looking and acting professionally. I always told my team, "You represent your school, your family, and your team; there is no more *me*." The same applies for the coach. When you realize this, it creates a sense of responsibility in everything you do.

  Always out-work your team because you're the leader. Be the first to work, the last to leave. Have everything planned and ready to go when the team arrives. Leave nothing to chance, whether it's paperwork, preparing for practice, scouting another team, or scheduling a game. When you take care of all the details, you allow your team to concentrate on what's important – practicing and playing the game. Never ask your team to do something you wouldn't do.

- **PROACTIVE/CONSISTENT** - Be a rock when making decisions. Hold a consistent line regardless of the situation, and whether it's a trivial or serious matter. When problems arise, take care of them quickly. Every decision you make will be scrutinized, especially those that involve key players or employees. Making exceptions will always come back to haunt you.

  Explain to your team in the first meeting that you will do your best to be fair in every decision but that there will be times when you can't be equal in deciding how to deal with a situation due to extenuating circumstances. Having a set of expectations for your team is a must.

- **BE HUMAN** - Admit it when you're wrong or make a bad decision. Show your team that taking responsibility is always best and that we all make mistakes. Modeling admission allows the team to see how to learn from a mistake, let it go, and move on.

- **SHOW PASSION**- Attend every seminar, clinic, and residential class or course possible. Become a member of your local and national organization. Be an active voice in the decision-making process of your sport or profession. If you want your team to improve, improve yourself. By doing this, you feed your love and passion for the game and come back renewed and eager to share new concepts and ideas. Your team will only be as passionate as you are.

- **CARE** - Be genuinely interested in the other talents of your players. Be a person they can turn to if they have a problem or situation that needs addressing. Players who know that you genuinely care about them, and their wellbeing, will always give you their maximum effort, whether in practice or the game. You will be amazed at the other talents your players have when they are allowed to share them. For instance, have a talent show night at the end of preseason, and enjoy it.

- **PROTECT/CELEBRATE** - Always step up and take responsibility for losses and miscues during a game, and gladly give all the credit to the team when they shine or win a contest. Allow them to enjoy their time on the team without being publicly blamed for mistakes. Respect your players, and talk to them away from the others if there are problems or issues. Work behind the scenes tirelessly for your players. Do everything possible to get them exposure, recognition, college visits, etc.

Concentrate on these five areas and respect for your team and your program will grow exponentially.

"Risk more than others think is safe. Care more than others think is wise. Dream more than others think is practical. Expect more than others think is possible." Claude Bissell

7

Nine Situations to Avoid During a Game

We represent our families, our schools and ourselves every time our team plays. That's a responsibility we shouldn't take lightly. All eyes are on us throughout a game with respect to our actions and how we respond during times of both adversity and jubilation.

Sometimes, during a game, we can be drawn into situations that can define our career in a negative way. Emotions on the sidelines run high in a tight game, especially against an opponent that has been a thorn in one's side for a long time. In the heat of the moment, it's easy to get caught up and do something that's out of character. While impacting the immediate game, it may also impact your ability to coach in the future. Likewise, it may affect how others define you.

We all have a responsibility to support our players to the fullest, but we need to think twice before stepping over that line. Here's a list of some situations to avoid:

- Loudly admonishing a player on the field who just made a mistake.

- Getting into a heated argument with your assistants.

- Making a loud, less than favorable comment about an opposing player.

- Getting personal with comments directed towards officials.

- Taking a phone call during the game.

- Addressing an upset parent.

- Laughing and joking with your players in a game that's already settled in your favor.

- Yelling at, or acknowledging, the opposing coach with disparaging remarks.

- Becoming engaged with opposing fans who are taunting you or your team.

My guess is that you've witnessed a few of the above situations, and possibly with coaches you wouldn't have expected such behavior from. When you become a coach at any level, you're a professional. Acting that way often requires some personal restraint. Always respect your players with comments directed towards helping them. Remember, they know they messed up. Instruct, or make comments, when they come out of the game or halftime.

- It's okay to disagree with assistant coaches. As a matter of fact, it's good. Just keep it civil and keep the heated arguments away from your players. Meet separately before addressing the team to work out the strategy. If you have differences, meet at a time away from the game.

- Never *ever* say anything derogatory about an opposing player during the game. You're an adult, so keep that in mind and be an example to your players. Should you hear your players saying something about an opposing player, address it immediately as inappropriate.

- If your reaction toward officials regresses to the point where you're making personal comments, you may be thrown out of the game. Would that help your team?

- Turn your phone off before the game. Unless you're waiting for a true emergency call, there is no need to have it on. Your #1 priority is the game and your players.

- It's rare, but should a parent come around to your bench during the game for anything other than a serious injury, or at the half, let them know firmly that you'll talk with them after the game. If necessary, address them away from the bench for a moment and let your assistants handle the game. Putting them off, or avoiding them completely, will only make matters worse. If they're enraged, you may have to get security to escort them away.

- A game that gets out of hand early, in your favor, can turn into a bad situation. Your players can lose focus and start laughing and acting silly on the sideline. Just remember, there's another team out there and they're watching. When you've been on the losing side of that game, as I have, you'll know what I mean.

- An opposing coach may yell in your direction if one of your players does something rash to a member of his/her team. Those remarks may not be very favorable. Avoid a shouting match, and understand anything you say won't make a difference at that moment. Talk with him or her after the game.

- Acknowledging opposing fans just gives them the fuel they need to continue harassing you and your team. Block them out mentally and stay focused on coaching your team. It's not really personal; you're just the opponent on that given night.

- If a game gets out of hand, with dangerous tackles flying in, there are actions you can take to protect your team. Stop the game and talk with the officials, the opposing coach, and Athletic Director. They may agree with your assessment that the game has gotten out of control. In that case, calling the game off, taking your team off the field to the locker room and home, is your best answer. A game is certainly not worth anything happening to your players.

While we may not see it at a particular moment, our actions can contribute to a game getting out of control. Before getting drawn into confrontation and unpleasantness consult with your assistants and get their opinions. Take a deep breath and think things through. Stay focused on your number one priority: the safety and well-being of your players.

8

Ten Lessons Coaches Should Never Teach a Player

Dear Coach,

I'll never forget the look on your face and the words that came pouring out when I made that mistake in the game. I knew the moment I made that decision that I had messed up and let the team down. Knowing they were counting on me at such a crucial time was tough enough, but to get blasted by someone I've looked up to all my life was really devastating. All I could do was sit quietly as my teammates and even the crowd heard every word you said.

I know it was in the heat of the moment in a huge game, and honestly I understand why you were upset. You had a right to be.

I've always wanted to be a coach when I graduate, and not even this incident will keep me from pursuing my dream.

You have, however, taught me 10 valuable lessons:

1. *There will be times when players make mistakes. They may even cost your team a win.*

2. *Walk away from your player if your emotions are out of control.*

3. *Words spoken in haste, with anger, can never be taken back.*

4. *Save the lecture for the locker room, away from everyone, even other players. This is a family (team) matter.*

5. *Make your point in a professional manner without attacking your player.*

6. *Always take the blame for your players in front of others when they ask.*

7. *When you ridicule a player in front of everyone, the relationship between you and your player will never be the same.*

8. *The play is over and done, all the yelling in the world won't change it. Work on what we will do now.*

9. *If you were out of control, apologize to everyone – the player, your team, the media, the school, your family – and let them know you were wrong.*

10. *Remember your players are devastated more than you will ever know before you say a word.*

Signed,

Your Player

*

Coaches often talk about being tough on players in an effort to get them ready for the next level (or life in general) and, in that context, I can agree it's needed daily in practice. However, in a game when players do something that is totally counter to what you've practiced or what they know is their responsibility, we have to remain composed. It's how we handle those moments that will impact their lives forever. It's not about winning or losing; it's so much bigger than that.

In the 1982 NCAA Men's Basketball Final game, Michael Jordan had just put North Carolina on top with 15 seconds to go. Georgetown raced the ball down the court in an effort to get the last shot to win the game. A Georgetown player inadvertently passed the ball to a North Carolina player thinking it was his teammate. North Carolina ran the clock out to win the title. I'll never forget Coach John Thompson of Georgetown with that signature towel draped over his shoulder seeking out his player who made the mistake and hugging him for the longest time. That's the model we need in our sports world today, a compassionate coach understanding what his player needed most at the time.

Ironically, Georgetown would win the title in 1984, and, yes, the player who made that mistake was on that team. You have to wonder… if Coach Thompson had lost his composure with that player, whether he would have still been on the team to contribute to the championship.

Remember, our players learn lessons from us every day from our actions and words. They can come from positive and negative situations. Let's make sure when it's learned from us, it's always positive, and they want to be like us for the right reasons.

9

Every Player Has a Role

Role Players... a term we often use for players with a specialized skill or limited ability.

Aren't all of our players 'role players'? After all, every player has a certain job or role to perform during the game. A defensive player's main objective may be to use their skills to pressure and win the ball, or contain the player in possession until help arrives. A striker's role may be to be relentless, create scoring opportunities, and beat defenders in key situations. But do we look at such individuals as role players?

In some sports, such as Football and Baseball, certain positions or responsibilities are clearly defined, but in soccer it isn't that easy. Generally speaking, if we have the ball, we're all on the attack and have to possess the skills and understanding to do so. The same is true for defending skills when we lose the ball.

Our so-called role players may see limited or no action depending on key game situations, but at some point in their careers they'll influence a game more that we can ever imagine…

We were playing a big city team that, for years, had viewed us as a warm-up game for bigger things. Their attitude was easy to detect, from the demeanor of their coach to the looks their players gave us as we warmed up.

We had bowed down and let them run over us during the previous season, but tonight would be different. We kept hanging around on the scoreboard and, as the horn sounded to end the game, the score was tied.

I've always loved to catch a glimpse of the other team in situations like this, and they were clearly upset with each other. This was on their field, and now the advantage was ours. We had nothing to lose and everything to gain as we headed into overtime. The two extra periods would prove nothing other than we had gained the momentum and had the opposition on their heels.

As overtime ended, the other team had a new look of doubt and almost respect that we had refused to go away. Now we were heading to penalty kicks where anything could and would happen.

It can be a challenge to strategically list your 10 shooters. We often overthink their order, leaving us to wonder if we made the right choices. Little did I know that it would go all the way to number 10 that night!

If it wasn't tense enough with the first five shooters, it was nerve-wrecking with the final five being 1 v 1 sudden death. After nine, it was still tied, and their tenth shooter had just missed. Our tenth shooter hadn't played a lot during the season. She was a great addition to our team from a chemistry and attitude point of view, but not the most skillful player we had. The scene was amazing - the whole team was encouraging and cheering for her. If she were to score we'd defeat a team we'd never beaten.

Her shot hit the back of the net, and our team went crazy piling on her and celebrating. I was so happy for her because this was her moment, and she'd always remember it. Who would have guessed she would win the game for us!

Is 'role player' just a politically correct term for substitute? I believe it is when we label them as such, have little faith in their complete ability in key situations, and only see them in a complementary role, thus limiting their playing time and contributions. Is that a fair assessment?

Not everyone on your team can be a starter. I do know that there are typically a number of players on any team who do not start but who we have confidence in (plus a few that we may not be so sure of). But at some point in their careers, they'll influence a game more than we can ever imagine…

It was a terrible night for a district championship game. Wind-driven rain was making the match almost unplayable. We were on our rivals' home field and it was a mess. The rain had soaked the field and puddles were everywhere. The game wore on without a score and the keepers were at a clear disadvantage with the ball skipping and picking up speed as it approached the goals. We had a freshman who had played very little, and who was playing up front in an effort to rest one of our veterans. One of our players crossed the ball and it landed like a golf ball on the green, not moving an inch. Our freshman poked the ball in the goal, and that's all we needed to win the championship. It was a true relief and certainly a moment she and her teammates will never forget. Who would have guessed she would win the game for us!

Evaluating highly skilled players is easy. The question becomes, what are our final criteria for keeping lesser-skilled players, and how can we develop them?

- **GRADE LEVEL** - Is there time to work with the player? With Seniors, the answer is usually no. With Juniors, one has to look closely. If they don't develop, you'll have to make a tough decision next season. With Sophomores, the big question to ask is did they progress as Freshmen? Your squad numbers may dictate keeping a player, but this can come back to haunt you. Consider how upperclassmen with potentially bad attitudes will influence your team more than younger players. I always ask myself 'could I put them in the game?' and seek the views of my assistants as well.

- **ATTITUDE** - Are they willing to make sacrifices and do what's best for the team (working hard in practice, but not seeing much playing time)? Once you keep a player, they expect to play (as do their parents). Players must have a purpose, something they contribute to the team. Be ready to share how they could contribute. It may be as simple as inspiring their teammates with a positive outlook, or developing a Big Sister/Little Sister Program, etc.

- **MOTIVATED** - Do they still have a passion for the game and want to improve. Are they willing to come in early or stay late to work on skills? Have a serious talk with them before you decide whether to keep them. What are their reasons for being there? If it's not 100%, by talking about it, they'll usually admit it and make the decision to leave. You may want to meet with their parents.

- **EXTRA SESSIONS** - Have your assistant coach set up times when players can work on individual skills. I would encourage all players to be there. Helping all players will strengthen your team, and give fringe players the motivation to improve.

- **SKILLS COACH** - Put players in contact with either a club coach, or a skills coach for individual attention. There are a lot of great coaches who focus entirely on this type of training. Parents are willing to spend money for their children's development, so take advantage of it.

- **YOUTH/CLUB COACH** - If possible, coach players in younger grades or club ball. This gives you an excellent opportunity to develop them and see their capabilities. Should you not have time, encourage your assistant to; or at the very least get to know their youth coach and have input on the player's development.

- **OPPORTUNITY** - Find a game or situations before or during the season to play your less skilled players. They need a chance to show what they can do, and you need to see it to truly believe in their ability. It may only confirm what you originally thought, but the players who still work to develop their skills had the opportunity, and I feel certain were appreciative of the chance, to contribute.

We spend a lot of time working with our key players knowing that everything they do will influence the game, and rightfully so. However, never neglect working with, and developing, your lesser-skilled players. Often, coaches will put young or lesser-skilled players on the other end of the pitch while working with their top players. That may work for you and your team, but remember as you gaze towards the far end, your season and success may depend on those players just as much as the stars on your team.

10

Eight Moments When a Coach's Impact Will Never Be Greater

Moments will define who you are as a coach, not wins or championships.

Every day, players look to their coaches for guidance for a variety of reasons including personal issues and crisis situations. Many of those will happen on or around the field or court. At that moment, we have the opportunity to make a positive difference in our players' lives. Here are eight situations you may encounter:

1. **PLAYERS' PERSONAL CRISIS** - Whether an injury, death in the family, or a problem the player can't handle, your priority should be to listen, and be there for them. Often, an injury ends the season, and a death is probably the first they've experienced. Let your assistants handle the team, then do anything you can for the player and their family. Coaching a game or practice pales into insignificance in comparison to these situations.

2. **A PLAYER'S MISTAKE COSTS A GAME** - During your career, you'll probably see one of your players make a mistake that costs your team. You can't change the moment or avoid it, but you can show compassion. Understand they'll remember this moment forever. Every player is different, just follow your heart with respect to your actions and let them know you will always believe in them. Remind them that one moment will never define who they really are.

3. **WINNING A CHAMPIONSHIP** - Winning brings its own set of challenges. That moment when the horn sounds or the last out is recorded is a moment when you'll have everyone's undivided attention. Parents, players and the community are waiting to hear your magical words. Let the emotion of the

moment guide you in a humble way. While applauding your team, make a special effort to mention the efforts of your opponent as well.

4. **COACHING MISTAKE** - We've all made mistakes during a game. All are obvious to us, and some are obvious to our players. If one of your mistakes costs your team a win or a championship, admit it. You don't have to apologize, just own it. Acting like it didn't happen, or you lost for another reason, degrades your character and integrity. Every move you make can't always end in a fairy tale ending, but never lose that willingness to make a bold move when your intuition tells you to.

5. **SUPPORTING A PLAYER** - A player, or a group of players, may come to you and complain about a certain player's ability or actions. This is often rooted in jealousy. It usually concerns the player who's getting all the outside recognition or scoring the majority of your goals. Stand strong for this player, letting the other players know no one player is more important than anyone else on the team, and that the player in question is doing exactly what the team needs. Remind them that those who know the game understand the efforts of every player to make possible a goal scored and how much you appreciate everything they do.

6. **LETTING A PLAYER GO** - One of the toughest tasks a coach has to deal with is cutting players in the preseason. Some coaches post lists, and never have any personal contact with those players. I think that is the wrong approach. Those players have worked hard and deserve a coach looking them in the eye as they let them go. The opportunity to make a positive impact on an uncomfortable situation is never greater. Respect those players and talk to every one of them.

7. **DEVASTATING LOSS** - Emotions can take over at a time like this, whether sad and tearful, or anger and disgust filled. When your players played as hard as possible, they probably are as upset as you. Put the loss on yourself, not them, whether it was their fault or not. Let them know how much they mean to you and that you appreciate everything they've done.

8. **DISCIPLINING ONE OF YOUR BEST PLAYERS** - When one of your key players does something unacceptable – forcing you to discipline them – keep in mind that everyone is watching

and waiting to see what you'll do. The expectations and rules are the same for everyone on your team. Never waiver in your responsibility to do your job. It may cost your team a win or even a championship, but softening the penalty or delaying it until after the game will cost you much more.

The responsibility of a coach is huge. Everyday situations arise that you may not have seen coming. Each one is unique and has the possibility to have a huge impact on your team. Doing your best to take advantage of a challenging situation and turning it into a moment that won't destroy a young person's confidence and self-image should always be your goal. Usually, there aren't any training sessions or video clips to guide you. It's just you and your heart and using your intuition to consistently do what's right.

11

How Do You Win Your Team Over?

There's nothing like coaching a team for the first time, whether it's your very first job, or if you've been around a while and are just taking over another team. How will you gain trust and convince your team that you have their best interests at heart? Why should they believe you're different from, better than, or as good as, the last coach they dealt with.

Parents and players in the audience don't care if your record is 300-0, you've coached 100 All-Americans, and won 7 National Titles. A successful past will certainly open many doors and extend your grace period but these parents and players are mainly concerned with what you can do for them in the *here and now*. That's why one of the keys to getting off to a great start is to gear your comments towards them, not your accomplishments.

Certainly, each situation is different. But a team that's had two or three coaches in a short span of time is often amongst the most challenging you could face. They will be callused to most of what you're saying… they've heard the speech before and have become skeptical. Can you blame them? It becomes paramount that everything you say can be translated into immediate, concrete actions that are visible to the team.

What will make you different?

1. **ACTIONS** - Everyone associated with the team will hear 50% of what you say, but will be watching 100% of the time to see if your actions are true to your words. If you know you can't deliver something, don't say you'll do it.

2. **CREDIBILITY** - Are you a coach of your word? Let players know as soon as possible if they aren't the right fit for your system, or if you don't see them playing much. Often upperclassmen from the previous year will still be on the team because the previous coach didn't want to make the decision to let them go. Never think that players will 'get the message' and

leave of their own accord. Be strong and let them know before it gets out of hand. Disgruntled players can destroy your team.

3. **HONESTY** - If you make a mistake, admit it. If you see something that isn't right, take care of it. Players need to know you'll stand up for them and make the right decisions based on expectations and values, not favorites.

4. **PROMISES** - This word should be used in a very meaningful way. Promises broken or never addressed will destroy your relationship with players and parents. A promise is an assurance that an expectation will be met.

5. **VISION** - Lay out your vision for the team, and begin work on it immediately. Mention it every day in how it relates to specifics during practice and games. The passion for that vision will spread to your players and continue to grow.

6. **WORK ETHIC** - Be a fireball of energy, passion and enthusiasm working at every chance. Be an example to your team and they will follow. Always outwork your team, and never have them do something you are unwilling to do.

7. **CONSISTENCY** - Never waiver in any decision with respect to expectations and discipline. Always be consistent. Players need to know you mean what you say. You can never make everyone happy, but you can base decisions on sound principles.

8. **COMMUNITY PROJECTS** - Get your team involved in important community projects. The chance to help others shows them life is more than a game. The sense of accomplishment in helping others as a team is a feeling that cannot be matched.

9. **INDIVIDUAL MEETINGS** - Nothing means more to a player than having a coach who is willing to sit down, listen and meet with them on an individual basis. This is a wonderful time to discuss individual goals, and how you can help make them a reality.

10. **TEAM BUILDING** - Take the time to use any and all team-building activities to bring your team together. If possible, take them on a ropes course. These are wonderful activities that challenge their decision-making, leadership, teamwork and physical ability. If they've had several coaches, they need that bond to tie them all together.

11. **TEACH, TEACH, TEACH** - At every opportunity, teach your players goal setting, a work ethic, expectations, motivation, personal discipline, nutrition, skills, tactical awareness, character, integrity, values, teamwork, leadership, respect, courtesy, humility, unselfishness, and more. You have a unique situation with a wonderful audience. Take advantage to make a difference in their lives.

It takes time for players from a team of many coaches to trust anything you say. There are no quick 'fast food' fixes. Don't rush things. Remember that every day is a building block for you to prove that you have their best interests at heart and that you'll do anything possible to help them be successful.

The beginning is always the most challenging. Selfish words from certain parents, an attitude from certain players, and the lack of skills and knowledge that you're used to, can be overwhelming. That's when your true colors will shine through. This team needs you. Never doubt that this is the place you need to be, and the joy of building this program will be one of the most rewarding aspects of your career. Anyone can coach a team of all-stars; the biggest challenge is to get them to play together. But show me a coach who can build a team from nothing, get them to believe in each other and accept their roles, and I'll show you a coach of the year.

There's a TV show that used the phrase, "You are being watched every hour of every day." It's an appropriate phrase as you begin a new coaching job. While you can't dwell on it, just keep in mind that your actions – not your words – will carry more weight with your players than anything else.

Section 2
Challenges

"When mentor leaders demonstrate their loyalty time and time again to those they lead – in both their personal and professional lives – those relationships will be fortified to withstand whatever challenges they face." Tony Dungy

We spend a lot of time researching the latest techniques and strategies for our game. Our offices are littered with books and DVDs so we can be ready for any situation during the game, or create excitement at practice. However, challenges are what we learn from the most (by experiencing them). They come in every shape, form, and fashion; usually at the most inopportune time.

What will you do when confronted by a player over a lack of playing time? How about dissension on your team? A fight? Failing grades? A player quitting? The list could go on and on. There will be many challenges throughout your career. Your ability to deal with these challenges, hold players accountable, and minimize the impact of these challenges on your team will determine your effectiveness. How will you learn to navigate troubled waters?

In this unit we delve into the following:

- Can you remain calm when confronted by an unexpected challenge?

- If confronted by a parent, will you feel the need to share all their son's or daughter's inadequacies?

- Have you ever fought for a player only to see them make the same mistake over and over?

- How will you deal with negative outside influences?

- What will you do with your team to minimize unwanted challenges?

- Is there someone you can turn to for help in times of trouble?

12

The Rough "C's"

When we're hired as a coach, we tend to think about the white collar aspects of coaching: championships, award banquets, developing All-Americans, personal recognition, and much more. It's only natural to have dreams of success, but the reality is that several barriers must be dealt with on our way to that dream.

That's why we need our blue collar too… lunch pail, hard hat, a roll-your-sleeves-up-and-grind-it-out-attitude to carry us through the four "C's" we'll encounter in our careers. Knowing the best way to navigate and deal with them is the key to how effective we'll be with our teams.

What are the "C's"?

- **CHOICES** - We might not view choices as an issue, but upon closer inspection, it becomes apparent why they lead the list. We're talking about choices between making decisions and not making decisions, doing what's right and what's not, standing up in times of struggle or not standing up, leading with values to help your players or not. Every choice you make as a coach defines who you really are and ultimately determines your impact on your team.

- **CONFLICT** - There's no way to avoid conflict with your team. In a season of high emotions, a competitive environment, and battling for positions there will be disagreements, squabbles, and arguments. Conflict can be positive if explained in the context of battling for a position on the team, and the life lesson of how to deal with it. Players need to understand conflict within the team only weakens it, and they need to find a way to work things out. As a coach, the need to jump right in may not be necessary during the early stages. Trust your players to deal with things. There will be time to get involved if needed.

- **CONFRONTATION** - When an issue is allowed to brew it can lead to a confrontation with ugly consequences such as shouting, yelling, and even physical fights. Whether on the field or off, fighting cannot be tolerated. The penalty must be severe.

Take your time gathering all the facts before finalizing your decision. Rightly or wrongly, it's clearly an issue that will define your team in other people's eyes. Getting the decision right is imperative!

- **CONTROVERSY -** Within your team, there may be opposing views on leadership, quality of play, and effort. Very often players group together on different sides of the issue leading to internal dissension. When this spills over onto social media (even prominent traditional media), it becomes costly to your team. Controversy usually requires strong leadership from either you as the coach or your administrator. Nothing good can come out of two groups squabbling during the season. It will destroy any team chemistry you have. At any hint of discord, jump in, get the parties together, listen to their positions, explain yours, and let them know in no uncertain terms that things must be resolved. If you feel inclined, you can give them a day to work it out, but my experience has been that this rarely works. Go ahead, be the bad person and make the decision. I'd rather them hate me than each other.

In every "C," your character and integrity gets called into question and comes under scrutiny. There are no easy answers, often anguish, and as we know… no way to make everyone happy.

Here are a few questions that may help guide you through any decision-making.

- **What do I know? Is there more?** Gather all the facts from those involved, those who were witnesses, and anyone who knew anything before the fact. Delegate some of the fact finding to your assistants if necessary.

- **What if I ignore this issue?** Often coaches tend to think, "What's the impact of dealing with this issue?" and that may be wrong. When you worry about consequences, they can cloud your judgment (e.g. sitting out a player for a big game, etc.). It's the decision not to deal with it which will impact your team much more. We've all seen coaches who delay a punishment against a top player until the big game is over. Decisions should never be based on how good a player is or what they do for the team.

- **Who am I making the decision for?** The decision is for the player and your team. Not for your boss, certainly not for you, public opinion, or anyone else. When expectations for conduct are in place and violated, the player must be held accountable.

- **Am I over-reacting?** Take the time necessary to absorb all the information. Making a decision in haste, especially when one isn't necessary when you're upset, and in the heat of the moment is not a good idea. Consult with your assistants to get their points of view.

- **Can I defend my decision?** When expectations and policies are in place, clearly explaining the rules, regulations, expectations and penalties for your team and school sees you able to defend your position. Remember to have everything in writing and have players sign a form stating that they received a copy of the rules of behavior before the season began.

- **What does my heart tell me?** Decisions are not easy, especially when a well-meaning player makes a mistake, but always make the decision. Deep down, your heart will tell you to do what's best for the team, and even that player will learn from the incident.

- **Will I be able to sleep at night knowing I made the right decision?** I heard a quote one time that said, "Doing the right thing is rarely easy." If you make the right decision, you can sleep well. It's only when you waiver, either in your ability to make a decision or in knowing you made the wrong decision for the wrong reason, that you will be kept up at night.

Your team is watching every decision you make. The ability to build Trust, Loyalty and earn their Respect will always be based on your sound judgments. Will you get every decision right? No. But when you've worked hard with your blue collar attitude, and it's based on sound character, integrity, and values, your players will know you did the best you could. This will keep your team on track to achieve their dreams.

13

Reaching the Un-Coachable

What comes to mind when you hear the term "un-coachable?" For most coaches, it conjures up negative images and a feeling of uneasiness. Have you ever had a player you would consider un-coachable? What did you do? Did it end with a heart-warming story, a parting of the ways, or just tolerance in an uncomfortable setting?

This is a topic that administrators often omit when teaching and training new coaches. Many would argue that experience is the best teacher, but at what cost to an individual or the team? Are there ways to "reach" the so-called un-coachable player? I believe there are, but first we need to explore how this player or players arrived at this point.

- **PARENTS** - Players are usually doing what their parents have taught them or what they expect them to do. If you've had a parent yell instructions which were totally opposite to what your team was trying to do during a game, you know what I mean. They may also be playing simply to please their parents even though it makes them miserable. In many cases, the player doesn't know how (or is unwilling) to tell their parents the truth. In truth, many players want to please their parents.

- **PREVIOUS/COMPETING COACH** - If you inherited a team from another coach or your players are also coached within another program in your off season, you may face challenges that arise from different styles and different philosophies. The problem may also be a lack of trust in coaches altogether based on previous encounters.

- **SUCCESS AT A LOWER LEVEL** - Players may have had success at a lower level where they were a premier player that gave them an over-inflated view of their ability based on playing inferior competition.

- **PERSONALITY** - Certain personalities may rub us the wrong way, especially players who are new to the system and don't mind saying something won't work in front of the team. Alternatively, those who are very passive may not provide any indication they are absorbing our advice on how they can improve.

- **UNDISCIPLINED** - Players may come to you having had free will over everything they did in their games with respect to conduct, decision making, communication, and punctuality; with no accountability.

- **KNOWLEDGE OF THE GAME** - There may be a case where a player has great ideas and an abundant knowledge of the game. While some coaches might feel threatened, we can use this to our advantage. It may just require teaching the player how to relate it in a professional way.

- **PERSONAL ISSUES** - There may be serious personal issues bothering the player, and they're simply acting out against authority or the team. If you suspect this is the case, get someone qualified from your school involved who can talk with the player in a professional setting.

- **BORED** - They may not be challenged enough in practice due to plans, lack of competition, or coaches who talk longer than they should.

There are certainly more situations than the ones I've mentioned. The key is finding out what underpins a player's apparent un-coachability and how best to handle it. Here are ten suggestions that may help.

1. **ASK QUESTIONS** - It may be as simple as asking a player why they play. If for instance, they're being pressured to play and don't enjoy the game anymore, I'd suggest talking with the parents or having the player talk with them.

2. **EXPECTATIONS** - Be very clear what you expect every day. While you may have gone over this with the team, it may require additional emphasis with this particular player.

3. **TALK INDIVIDUALLY** - If a player does something that is out of line, grab your assistant coach and the player and talk with them. Let them know you won't tolerate whatever it is, and what behavior you expect. Having the assistant involved sends a signal to the player that expectations will be enforced consistently and provides a witness to what was said.

4. **PAIR WITH A STRONG TEAM LEADER** - Put the un-coachable player with your strongest team leader in every situation possible. Let them see a model of behavior and responsibility, and the respect that is earned.

5. **BUILD TRUST** - Treat them with the same respect you expect from them. Build trust every day with your decisions and actions.

6. **BE FIRM** - Should a player cross a line, be firm in what your discipline policy requires. Wavering will only make things worse, and respect will be lost.

7. **EXPLAIN BENEFITS** - Take the time to explain all the individual benefits of being part of the team and where it could lead them individually with respect to playing at the next level.

8. **CHALLENGE** - Put them in challenging situations in every practice with numbers down (1 v 2), (2 v 3), etc. or match them up with the least-skilled players on their team. Whatever it takes, make them use their skill to its fullest to succeed. Allow them the opportunity to show you how skilled they are.

9. **LEADERSHIP ROLE** - Share with them the possibility of a leadership role on the team that can be earned through strong character traits, classroom achievement, and helping teammates.

10. **FREEDOM IN CERTAIN SITUATIONS** - Give your player the freedom to be themselves in certain situations, whether it's corner kicks, free kicks, or taking someone on in the 18-yard box. Let them know you trust their judgment in those situations.

You have several choices with the "un-coachable" player. Tolerate them in an uncomfortable setting and watch it destroy your team, spend all your time correcting them and neglect the rest of your team, or give them clear guidelines that apply to everyone on the team and let them decide – through their actions – what direction they want to go.

We can't change our coaching style for every new player that comes into our system, but we can recognize the situation and do our best to shape a player into the best individual they can become. Ultimately, when you've laid it out there and made every effort, the choice resides with the player.

In my opinion, the term "un-coachable" puts it all on the coach. However, if I've done all I can to transform this player and they are still resistant then it's on them and maybe the term should be unplayable.

14

Negativity... Easy to Spot, Tough to Deal With

Every day, subtle hints are there to alert you that negativity is trying its best to surface within your team. The cause could be evident in someone's actions, by the lack of effort they put into work, their attitude, or by certain groups not associating with others.

While most may be minor issues that require little involvement, others – if left unattended – can disrupt team chemistry, jeopardizing the next game or the season. How do they get started? It may be as simple as a statement by one of your players, an assistant coach, administrator, parent, or even you. Yes, you. Often we have to pull ourselves out of a negative situation, and think, "What did I just say?"

"Remember, not everyone on your team wants to win that championship," a veteran coach once shared with me at a clinic.

"Are you serious?" I said. "We're a team, and it benefits everyone. I understand how our opposition and rivals would be pulling against us, but our own players? No way!"

How would you react to the above conversation? Would you say, "Who is it? I'll get rid of them!" That might be your impulse but is it really that easy?

We spend a lot of time training coaches and players to be positive; providing an affirmative environment that promotes healthy competition and teaches life lessons. As we do, negativity seems to slip in and out because we aren't prepared to deal with it. Sometimes we overreact, which puts us on the same level as those who are only concerned about their own special interests.

What creates an atmosphere that helps negativity to grow? By their nature, sports programs are fertile ground.

- **INCONSISTENT/NO LEADERSHIP** – A failure to recognize negativity, the hope that it will all go away, and the inability to make tough decisions. Players want shared leadership until the decision is tough, then they expect you to make it. Step up and lead.

- **NO CLEAR EXPECTATIONS** - A team without expectations is making the rules up as they go along, and often based on selfish, individual interests.

- **POSTURING FOR POWER** - Often those who have been in charge or who have played certain positions make their views known to all new players in a way that discourages new ideas, enthusiasm, even an ability to play a particular position.

- **CLIQUES** - Many teams will have groups that exclude others from their special club. This may lead to bullying and victimization.

- **FAVORITISM** - Coaches may contribute to negativity by continually highlighting a certain player or players (and, in particular, flaws) in conversations/media.

- **OUTSIDE INFLUENCES** - While you have little control over this area, be aware that others may be feeding your players negative ideas/thoughts.

- **RUMORS/INNUENDO** - Someone on your team may start a rumor to disrupt another player's success, or blame them for something they had nothing to do with.

- **WORTHLESS TRADITIONS** - Often players will have something they carry from a former team that undercuts what you're trying to accomplish. "We tried that but it never worked," or "We've always done it that way."

How can you deal with these issues?

- **CONSISTENT LEADERSHIP** - Step up promptly, and make decisions based on what's best for the team and in line with the expectations that are laid out at the beginning of the season. The players should hold each other accountable. When they are reluctant, remember your responsibility as a leader to act.

- **ESTABLISH PLAYER EXPECTATIONS** - Work with your players to establish strong expectations that guide your team in challenging times concerning behavior/commitment. If they're involved in the process, expectations are no longer simply *your* rules, but ones that are important to them.

- **NO CLIQUES** - Be crystal clear concerning the fact that you are all a team. It doesn't mean you'll always agree with each other, but it does mean you support each other on the field and during team activities. Stress that we all have certain friends we hang out with more than others, but we never exclude others in hateful, demeaning ways because of who they are or what they believe.

- **MEET WITH PARENTS/ADMINISTRATORS** - Engage with those associated with the program and explain how much you need their help in motivating and supporting players and everything the team is trying to do. Remind them of your philosophy with respect to providing a positive environment that promotes success.

- **BIG SISTER/LITTLE SISTER, BIG BROTHER/LITTLE BROTHER** - Nothing is better than putting new players with positive upperclassmen. It gives the upperclassmen the satisfaction of giving something back to the program, and the new player really feels wanted in a new setting. Mentoring is a great idea for building your program.

- **COMMUNITY SERVICE** - This is a great way to keep your team grounded in what's really important during the year. Helping those who might not be able to help themselves may be just what your players need to shed their selfish attitudes.

- **BUILD TRUST/RESPECT** - Understand that every decision, every situation, every practice, every game you're involved in is under constant scrutiny from your players, parents, and administrators. The trust you build with your team comes from decisions you have to make. You may not get them all right, but be willing to admit it when you don't. Earning each other's trust and respect is a big key to becoming a successful team.

- **TEAM BUILDING** - Putting players in challenging situations outside the game allows them to see each other in a different light. They may gain a new respect for each other. Often players who struggle in the game can excel over rope courses, physical challenges, etc., and in some situations leaders will step forward who might have otherwise been left unnoticed. Bringing your team together at every opportunity is always a good idea.

- **LEADERSHIP COUNCIL** - Establish a Leadership Council at your school with representatives from each sport. Allow athletes and coaches to explore ideas to combat problems common to every team. Sharing challenges and solutions makes every program better.

- **NO DISSENSION** - Do your best to find the reason behind any dissension on your team. Talk to the parties involved separately, then bring them together to find a solution. Remind them of how much they mean to the team and others that count on them. If one is clearly the aggressor, and creating an unhealthy environment, then a suspension or expulsion from the team may be for the best.

Building a program requires strong leadership that is shared with your players. It's a building block for the foundation of your program. Work diligently at every practice, every game, and with those you come into contact with, to keep negativity locked out.

Never confuse complaining about working hard, or learning something new, with negativity. These are natural reactions that stem from being moved out of a comfort zone. Players can become content in a comfortable world that doesn't require a lot of effort, and which doesn't push them to do more than they've ever done. Once the benefit is seen, the complaints usually fade away.

It's the deep down signs of negativity, as previously mentioned, that really destroy a team or individual player. We should be able to recognize and deal with them.

Your conviction and your passion will be tested every day. Stay true to the vision you have for the program, share it with your players, and focus on what you can control.

Negativity, while not something we hope to deal with, reminds us of our mission to lead our players in a proper way to a place they've never been. It will be worth it.

15
Coaching Storms

Vacations are a wonderful time to relax and enjoy lovely surroundings. Planning a vacation is often a terrific period: full of excitement and anticipation. You can picture the scenic venues, beautiful weather, and wonderful times ahead. It's impossible to see anything else.

Often, though, unexpected weather moves in and spoils our plans, or a family member gets sick and extra holiday effort is required. Certainly not what we had planned, but it happens.

Coaching is a lot like the above. We plan with great joy, looking forward to a successful season with our team. You can't help but think ahead to the big matchups with top teams and winning the post-season tournaments, alongside working with all the great players you have returning that year. Most of us can't wait for opening day. It's what we live for.

You would think we would temper our excitement after several seasons knowing what may happen during the year. But, as a coach, the best thing you can have is a short memory. It can help when times become challenging.

What storms could we encounter this year?

1. Dissension
2. Injuries
3. Concerned Administrators
4. Complacency
5. Disruptive Behavior
6. Unhappy Parents

How can we deal with them, making sure they don't linger and have a bigger impact on our season than necessary?

Bringing your team together to determine their goals is a key ingredient for a successful season. Be clear with your expectations, and allow the team to be involved in establishing them. Often players will have their own agenda or be a distraction to the rest of the team. It's imperative you recognize this and take action. Don't let things linger and hope they will improve. Talk to that player or group of players. I love this line from Gregg Popovich of the San Antonio Spurs, "No one is bigger than the team. If you can't do things our way, you're not getting time here and we don't care who you are." We get what we allow.

Injuries aren't something you can control, so worrying about them before they happen is fruitless. When they occur, support your player(s) during their time away from the game. If that involves going to the hospital, do it. Reassure them – when appropriate – that everything will be okay. Your team may need reassurance as well, that their goals are still attainable even without a key player.

Administrators can be a distraction if they (or others around them) have dropped hints, or told you directly your job may be in jeopardy. Honestly, this is a distraction you may live with every year. It should always be a big motivator to constantly do your best. As a coach, your job is always in peril, and the risk of being let go is part of the profession.

Teams who've won championships the year before can become complacent. They lose sight of what they did to accomplish their goals. Convincing them of what it will take to repeat a successful season can be a monumental job.

We had just won the regional tournament by beating our cross-town rival in a shootout. The feeling was one you just can't describe. I was so proud of our team and what they'd just done. As we lined up for pictures with the trophy, a thought kept finding its way into my mind: we are moving to a tougher district next year. How would that impact upon our ability to succeed? The following year I did my best to remind the players, every day, of what we were facing but they refused to buy in and work harder and smarter to have a chance. We would exit the tournament early because our team had become complacent and content with last year's success. As a coach, I had let my team down because we encountered a storm I was unable to deal with.

Discipline is an area you have to be ready for at any time. It can be minor or major. One thing to keep in mind is not to make it a bigger deal than necessary. Whatever the expectation or rule is, enforce it and move on. Don't make it personal or berate a player. Everyone makes mistakes, but we all must face the consequences of our actions. The keys to discipline are consistency and fairness. Players need to see you'll be consistent regardless of whomever the player is and that you'll be fair in the punishment.

Parents are a huge asset, often spending countless hours fundraising, working concessions, and more, for your team. They can also roll in like a big summer storm at any time. The number one issue is playing time for their child. As the game progresses and they sit in the stands with other parents whose children are playing, the anger grows. Then after the game they may seek you out. You can do your best to avoid this situation by addressing it at preseason parent meetings. Make clear your position on playing time and talk about it. Explain when you'll be happy to meet with parents.

I know coaches who flat out tell parents, "I won't talk about playing time." If that's your philosophy, let the parents know. Personally, I've never said that because I'd rather meet with a parent at an appropriate time than have them stewing about it all year long. If you're confident in what you're doing, there's never a reason to avoid someone. I would recommend a 24-hour rule for parents. They're required to wait 24 hours after a game to set up a meeting with you. It's also prudent to address social media rules with respect to emails, Twitter, Facebook, Instagram, etc. and the need to refrain from comments about players and coaches.

As the season begins, you may see big clouds on the horizon only for them disappear in an instant. There may be other clouds that roll in under the radar without warning. Your ability to deal with these storms will have a huge impact on your season. Maintaining a calm demeanor when times are tough is a great asset. Your players and parents need to see you're in control and not rattled.

There will be seasons when storms are almost non-existent, and other seasons when it seems they'll never end. Be thankful for the tough seasons, they're the ones that define your character and what you stand for.

Remember, anyone can coach your team when the skies are clear.

16

Dissension... Are You Contributing?

Whether you've coached or played, you will inevitably have experienced dissension. You know what I'm talking about: that time when a player (or players) disrupts the team's road to success with individual wants and needs.

I must admit nothing irritates me more than a selfish player, especially when it's so obvious. But could we, as coaches, be contributing to the problem?

I've worked with many bosses and played for several coaches over my career. Many had outstanding qualities that I admired and which I tried to emulate. Several could have led any group into the toughest conditions, and the group would have followed them unconditionally.

On the other hand, some of my bosses created an environment of dissension by always highlighting their favorite employees or players in meetings and communications. I believe we often do that (sometimes without even realizing it) as coaches.

I've observed coaches who continually hold one, two, or a group of players up to the rest of the team. They even shout from the sideline, "Pass the ball like Julie!" or "Win the ball back, Michael can do it!" While the comment may appear to be a challenge to a player, it can also be taken as a put down in front of the team.

Our mission is to bring together a group of players with varying backgrounds, skills, talent, and personalities. Over the course of some seasons, this seems to naturally come together, while other seasons prove far more challenging with unique situations brought on by what appears to be selfish wants and needs. Are we feeding the situation?

We may not be as vocal or as obvious as the examples previously mentioned, but favoritism can be perceived through our demeanor at practice or a game. I've heard some coaches say, "I treat every player the same." That seems like an easy solution, but is it possible? I don't think it is.

Our personalities tend to be more receptive to certain players, and we feel comfortable talking with, and being around, those individuals. Where does that leave us? We can't change for every player, and I wouldn't want every player to change just for me. I do, however, believe we can diminish the possibility of dissension by carefully thinking about how we act, our body language, and what we verbalize.

There's no doubt that all coaches have favorite players who display high skill levels, dedication, fearlessness, commitment, etc., and we admire them. The key is not to throw that in the other players' faces. Rather, find someone outside the team (such as a professional player) for them to emulate.

If you rank your players' abilities with respect to fitness, skills, or some other criteria, it paints a crystal clear picture of who the best player is. There's no need for you to boast about that player or hold that player in the highest esteem in front of everyone else. However, if you need to make a particular point, and it surrounds a particular individual, do not go on and on about this player, and be sure to mention other players as well.

There's not a player on your team who doesn't know who the best player is. I'm sure many wish and dream of becoming as good as they are. In that respect, they want exactly what you want. When you remember this, it brings you to the reality that there's no need to blast them with another team member's name.

Everyone on your team is important and has a role, or you wouldn't have kept them. The key is communicating in a thoughtful way the importance of that role and how the success of your team depends on every player.

Dissension may appear during a season, but it need not come from us.

17

What Will You Say?

We had fought the entire game with everything we had. We were clearly outmatched, especially in terms of being able to score. Our plan at this point, in the regional championship during second overtime, was to extend the game to penalty kicks and take our chances there. I felt very confident that our goalkeeper would be the difference when it came to penalties. They had a wonderfully gifted player that we had marked the entire game. She was frustrated and unable to shake loose for a chance to put one in.

We were playing one of our best games at the right time. Our players on the sideline were cheering their teammates on. With about 5 minutes left, I was still on edge realizing that at any point they could score, but our team was refusing to let that happen. Left unmarked, one of their wing players struck a ball right in front of our bench toward the goal. It sailed over our goalkeeper's head into the upper corner of the goal. A beautiful goal if you weren't anyone associated with our team. It was all they needed, and we lost the game to our fiercest rival. It was heartbreaking.

One thing I pride myself on is that my teams never fall or collapse to the ground in anguish over a loss. We deal with a loss in the best way we can, and always line up to shake hands. There will be plenty of time for sadness and tears on the way home.

What do you say to your team when they give everything they have and still come up short?

In those moments, I believe we should:

1. Let the players know how very proud we are of them and their effort and determination.
2. Be brief. Save the speech for the banquet.
3. Place no blame, other than on yourself.
4. Show your heart is broken as well. It's okay to cry.

5. Take time to visit the team as a group, as well as with each player.

6. Recall with them how special the season has been.

7. Silence is golden, just sitting or being alongside players is sometimes enough.

8. When it's a season-ending loss, express gratitude and appreciation towards your seniors.

9. Learn how to deal with a loss as a coach. Players are more resilient than we are, and let go of things quicker. There will be other games to coach.

It was, in most of our minds, a game we were expected to win. We had defeated this team in a preseason scrimmage, and a regular season game. This was the regional semifinals. Everyone knew we'd meet our crosstown rival in the finals on Saturday. No one was taking them for granted, but we knew we had the talent to win, especially being in this game for the first time in recent years. The problem was, no one told the other team. They were all over us, clearly the best team on that night. We just couldn't get anything going, and missed shot after shot.

Falling behind by a goal in the second half put us on the attack, but the more we tried, the less effective we were. The horn sounded, and disbelief was written all over our faces as the other team celebrated on the field. We shook hands and headed to a corner away from the field. Our players, especially our seniors, were visibly shaken realizing this was their last game.

A few years back, our players had seemed immune or indifferent to showing heartfelt emotion and tears after a season-ending loss. My assistant coach always reminded me of that, and said it showed the game didn't really mean much to them. I never liked that statement, but knew she was right. However, on this particular night, I saw much more. It did mean something to the majority of players. As their tears and mine ran down our faces I knew as a coach (as did my staff) that we had accomplished something much more important than winning a game. We created a team that truly understood what sacrifice, commitment, dedication and, yes, even heartbreak meant.

18

How Can You Save
A Team in Decline?

Are you able to recognize a team in decline, particularly if the indicators are less than obvious? What a crazy question! Most of us would answer with a resounding yes, but are there times when we might not see them. Or we avoid recognizing them because we hope they will go away. Or we feel the signs don't really mean anything.

When our teams are successful, it's easy to get wrapped up in the moment and fail to see farther down the road. I agree we should enjoy the moment – when things are going right – but should always be planning and calculating for the next game, next season, and even three years from now. We need to ensure that decline doesn't happen or that, at best, we can minimize it.

There are obvious indicators of a team in decline:

- A low number of players. Very few players are trying out.

- The talent pool at lower levels is decreasing or transferring.

- Very little player enthusiasm or passion.

- Lack of effort during the game.

- Practice feels more like punishment than working on skills and situations.

- No plans for next season with respect to off-season player development.

- Not just losing, but losing in an embarrassing way.

- The coach's decision-making is consistently questionable.

There are also some more subtle indicators:

- Softening the schedule so as to keep the win total respectable.

- Younger players are not gaining any game experience.

- Not as successful against mediocre opponents.

- Coach is working but has lost all enthusiasm.

- Players not as prepared mentally and physically for the game as in the past.

- The attitude of players and coaches; living off past successes.

- Coach is pressing for answers in the game, not practice.

- Players are questioning the coach's decisions.

One of the most flawed indicators that we've left off the list is the win/loss record. While a lot of people look at this and immediately see a team in decline, that may not always be the case. The win/loss record may not appear as good as for a previous season, but there may be positive or uncontrollable reasons for this. The coach may have toughened the schedule up with stronger teams, a key player or players may be injured, or the coach may be mixing veterans with younger players to get them ready for a run in a tournament.

A team in decline is a terrible affliction that most coaches fear. Some aspects of this may be unavoidable, such as an ebbing and flowing talent pool (especially at the high school level). For college teams, it may be reflected by the loss of players who were expected to sign. However, I know you'll agree that we have control over 99% of the rest. So, how do we make sure our team is immune to decline?

Here are some ideas that will make a difference:

- Create a positive environment that players want to be in.

- Challenge your players every day.

- Come to practice and games with a contagious spirit and passion.

- Refuse to give in to negativity and setbacks.

- Sell your program to everyone you meet.

- Help coach younger players, or at least meet them when they play.

- Attend every clinic and seminar possible.

- Be positive with your players and allow them to make mistakes.

- Build character and integrity in every practice and game situation.

- Allow your players to lead.

- Conduct a camp for all age groups.

- Take the blame when possible, and give credit to your players.

- Be consistent in every decision.

- Be there for your players when there's a problem which doesn't involve the game.

By doing everything we've mentioned, and more, you'll be the coach that everyone wants their child to play for. It will take hard work and dedication, but it will (at worst) minimize your team's decline and (at best) continue to improve it. There will be challenges along the way, but you'll be in a position to consistently compete with any team you play year after year.

A decline may be inevitable is some situations. Your responsibility will be to recognize it, and lead your team to a more successful place.

19

What Will You Do When the Game is On the Line?

What do your players see when they come to you before a key moment in a game? Are you cold, calculated, calm, confident? Or out of control, yelling, confused-looking, and communicating too much information (that's often not even relevant)?

Are you prepared for this key moment? What will you do?

From the movie Hoosiers.

During a timeout near the end of the state championship game, Coach Norman tells the team they'll use Jimmy, their best player, as a decoy, and Merle will take the final shot. The team is visibly upset. Coach Norman looks around and asks, "What's the matter with you guys?" Jimmy looks at Coach Norman and says, "Don't worry, coach, I'll make it." The revised play works with perfection, and they win the game.

While the movie is loosely based on the Milan High School team that won the 1954 Indiana State Basketball Championship (they did win with a last second shot), it reminds us of our role as a coach at key moments. Are we able to listen and consider our players' ideas? After all, they've worked the whole game against this opponent and have a feel for what will be successful.

How do you decide on the game plan when your players are looking to you for some magic? There are many factors to consider. Here are a few that relate to basketball:

- The situation.

- What are our strengths?

- Input from your assistants and players.

- What players do we need?

- Very specific instructions to the players.

- How many options do we have time for, off this setup?

- Go for the tie or the win? What are the percentages?

- When we score and there's still time on the clock, we _____.

- _____ takes the ball out of bounds?

- _____ takes the inbound pass to start the play?

- If we should miss, we _____.

Many sports, such as baseball, softball, basketball and football to name a few, allow coaches to control the game. Their use of numerous timeouts, called plays, and stoppages let coaches do their best to influence the outcome. It's when they're out of timeouts or down to their last out that you see how good the coach is. The game is on the line.

Other sports, such as soccer, offer coaches rather less control during the game. So, how can soccer coaches influence the game in the final minutes, overtime, or a shoot-out?

Coaches and players who've been successful in critical situations will readily tell you they'd prepared for that moment all their lives. Many have never been in that exact situation, of course, so how could they say that? Here are a few traits they all have:

- **CONFIDENCE** - They know they're going to win.

- **RELAXED** - The moment is in slow motion to them.

- **VISION** - They've hit the shot, or set up the play a thousand times.

- **MENTALLY STRONG** - Willing to lose to win; resilience.

- **DETERMINED** - Will do anything it takes.

- **ENJOY THE MOMENT** - They relish the crowd and noise.

- **WANT THE BALL** - They want to carry or lead their team.

Hall of Fame Football Coach John Madden and his Oakland Raiders were playing the Baltimore Colts in a playoff game. Oakland had a third and long, needing least a field goal to tie the game. Coach Madden was an excitable guy on the sideline and called a timeout. As quarterback Ken Stabler came to the sideline, Madden was getting information from his assistants and coming up with the play. Stabler cocked his helmet back and gazed at a rowdy sellout crowd and said,

"Wow! The fans are getting their money's worth today." Madden relaxed knowing Stabler had the confidence to win the game. On the next play, he hit Dave Casper with a pass putting them in position for the field goal that tied the game, sending it to overtime, which Oakland won.

We've all had Kenny Stablers in our careers. They're very special. Do we always recognize them? In some instances, I believe not. We may want to come up with the big play involving an unproven player, or ask our star to do something that plays against their strengths because of our ego. Overcoaching can often lead to failure or lost confidence from our players. The best recourse is to utilize your talent.

As a young coach, I felt I knew everything about the game of soccer and wanted to put my team in a position to win every night we played. On one particular night, we'd fought our way into overtime and then a shoot-out against a superior opponent. As we got ready for the shoot-out there were so many things I wanted to go over and say to our players (reminders of placement, disguise, etc.).

Looking back, the players knew where I was going and could sense my nervousness. One of our leaders raised her hand, and when I acknowledged her, she simply looked me in the eye and said, "Coach give us the shooters, we got this. Remember you've prepared us for this moment every day." A cold calm came over me, and I knew she was right. We would go on to win the game, but more importantly, I learned a lesson that day. *Prepare your players and then trust them.*

During a recent timeout in a NCAA tournament basketball game, the coach was silent, allowing the players to work out what adjustments were needed to get them back on track. This was a veteran coach that had been in this position before, and the plan worked. While most of us might not go that far, especially with a young team, such a move will empower players and make them accountable. It's a positive step in building the trust between a coach and his or her players that can lead to success.

As you plan for those final moments in the big game, remember your best resource… your players!

20

Dealing with that Last Loss

How do you handle that season-ending loss? I'm not talking about addressing your players or your team. I mean, how do you *personally* deal with it? Many coaches have shared with me how it's one of the toughest times of the season.

Everything comes to a screeching halt. No more practices to plan. No more bus requests. No more interviews, no more games, no more demands. As coaches, we all thrive on demands and challenges. Days off, or when the season ends, are tough. So what now?

For most of us, it's like a heavy fog has moved in and all our coaching energy has dissipated. Often we head down that "should have, could have, what if" road.

You know the one.

That imaginary dirt road littered with dusty championship trophies that have our team's name on them. It's also the one where you beat yourself up with thoughts of, "Did we really lose?" or "What if that goal had gone in?" or "I should have made this adjustment". And the one thought we can't get out of our heads is, "I've let my team down." It's something we all do, but it's wasted energy draining our ability to function.

So can we avoid this situation completely? I don't think so. If the game and your team mean anything to you, you'll have these thoughts when you lose and the season ends. The better question may be, "What can I do to reduce the length of time I feel this way?"

Many coaches take vacations directly after the season to completely get away and recharge their batteries. Personally, I've found you can't escape your emotions and thoughts even if you're halfway around the world.

So here are my suggestions:

1. **ROUTINE** - Looking any loss 'right in the eye' may be your best therapy. You'll find top level coaches in their office the day after their season ends. In their view, it serves no purpose to

feel sorry for themselves or their team. After all, you're the leader, and you have to remain strong even when it's tough. It doesn't mean the loss doesn't hurt. It's just one way of competing with it. Keeping a routine, even when the season ends, is one of the best things you can do. It gives you purpose and hope for next season. You certainly won't have as much to do – compared to when the season was still ongoing – but it's enough to get you through this tough time. Take the time you would spend practicing and work on next season.

2. **PLANNING** - Take what you learned from the loss and use it to your advantage in planning practice sessions and what you want to accomplish next year. Work on your schedule. Plan your own camps or camps that your team will attend. Add some variety to your schedule such as a weekend trip against some top teams. Research new team building activities for ropes courses, or white water rafting. Also, think about some Friday night cookouts. These will bring a smile to your face as you think about all the players you have coming back, and what your team can accomplish.

3. **FEED YOUR PASSION** - Attend as many clinics, conventions or residential courses as possible. If you haven't already, plan to get the highest level license or diploma in your sport. Spending time with your colleagues will teach you many lessons (not least of which that all coaches experience setbacks as well as wonderful moments!). It's also a great time to share strategies and ideas that have worked or failed miserably. Your passion batteries will be recharged in this setting and, more importantly, you'll see you're not alone in anything you've experienced.

4. **PROMOTE/ASSIST** - Set up speaking engagements with your local organizations promoting your program and get your team involved with charity events or businesses that need volunteers. Nothing shows us how unimportant winning or losing a game is when helping those who need our assistance, and the joy or gratitude that brings. The lessons learned in this setting will last you and your players a lifetime.

5. **MEET WITH YOUR TEAM** - Meet with your team as soon as possible to detail plans you have for next season. They will also be experiencing a range of emotions from the season's end. Let them plan or create some of the activities for next year. They need a sense of purpose and relief as well. Talk with your young players and those in the feeder system of your program.

Let them know how excited you are about them joining your team.

6. **VACATION** - I know, I know. Earlier, I wrote how you cannot escape the emotions of losing after the season. I still stand behind that statement, but the key is timing. Wait until you've established something of a routine and got over the sting. You'll enjoy your vacation with those who care about you most when the dust has settled, and you're thinking about next season with a smile and fresh possibilities.

Every coach is different. We all have to deal with that season-ending loss in our unique way. None of us wants it to happen, and it's hard not to take it personally. Often our players have no idea of the anguish we feel at that moment. But just like our players, we are resilient; we just don't bounce back as quickly.

Experience can help, but it's no cure. There aren't any quick fixes or solutions, just the knowledge that we'll get through it. Getting back up and into your routine will bring about a renewed passion for next season. That energy will come back strongly as you realize you have the greatest job in the world!

21

What Makes You Think…

A year off can make a huge difference. Back in 2007, I had resigned from a program that meant everything to me. I built it from its birth into a potential powerhouse that was ready to explode, but knew resigning was the right thing to do as I faced back surgery. I wanted to make sure my physical challenge didn't affect the team in any way and, if I couldn't do something 100%, I would step aside.

The surgery went well with no physical limitations but during my year away, my former team flourished, and I caught myself missing being on the sidelines. As I completed my recuperation, it soon became clear that our cross-town rival needed a coach, and the parents asked if I would take the job. After talking with my wife, I jumped at the opportunity.

At the first parent meeting, I was drilled with pointed questions as though I were a first-year coach, especially from one parent. It caught me off guard since I'd been very successful in coaching my former team for 14 years.

The questions ranged from whether or not I was going to coach the middle school team, why I took the job, was I physically able and if we were going to practice twice a day. There was also the unspoken question (which pervaded many others) as to what made me think I could coach this team. The lead inquisitor let me and everyone in the room know that his daughter was the middle school's MVP the previous year, as a sixth grader, and scored the most goals.

All this had come before I had the chance to address the group with my goals and philosophy. As I was given the chance to speak, I explained my philosophy and plans for the coming season, which included my disdain for individual awards, especially in a team game. That stance would eventually cost our team a future player, but I believed in my philosophy then, and I believe in it now.

I knew my work was cut out for me.

I coached the middle school program because I wanted to get to know the players, and them me. If you get the chance, do it. Imprint your philosophy on the younger players and parents so they'll have an understanding of what to expect as their daughters or sons progress. We had a terrific middle school team and a terrific year. At that point, the future was bright for our high school program with this group of players moving up.

During that summer, the parent mentioned above called me while I was on vacation to let me know they were transferring to our cross-town rival's middle school. I told him I wished his daughter the best and said goodbye.

Remember, this was middle school soccer! His attitude over the phone was as though it was a college choice and it had come down to the other school. Before her career was over, the player would leave that school and transfer one more time, being unhappy with their staff like her father was with me and mine. Ironically, she would end up winning a state championship with her last team, and I was glad because she was a terrific player and a fierce competitor.

I understand a parent has the right and responsibility to do what's best for their child, and I respect that tremendously. As a coach, I only want players and families who believe in what we're doing and who want to play for us. You can only coach the players in front of you. In our situation at the high school level, recruiting is illegal, so your players are limited to those walking your halls.

My concern is this: What lessons are we teaching our children when we move them from program to program for the sake of either individual or team awards? What will happen when they're adults making decisions with their families about their jobs?

What makes you think you're qualified to coach my child?

In my case, taking away the MVP award (and other individual awards) was part of the reason our team lost a player. But what traits are parents looking for in a coach? I think it varies with what the parent's goals are.

Parents who want their child to play in college usually favor a coach who:

1. Has a strong pedigree in the sport - someone who has played at the highest level.

2. Is knowledgeable - able to conduct a thorough practice and coach the game.

3. Teaches individual skills - makes their son or daughter a better player.

4. Is a driver - tough and demanding.

5. Is a disciplinarian - has control of the team.

6. Has connections - has college contacts for scholarships and exposure.

7. Is also focused on the offseason - requires the player to work year round exclusively on their sport.

Parents who want their child to be part of a team and learn the social and physical dynamics of a sporting experience may want a coach who:

1. Has played the game.

2. Is competent enough to conduct practice and coach the game.

3. Has a caring attitude about every player.

4. Is willing to help the player improve.

5. Rarely raises their voice.

6. Makes a conscious effort to get everyone in the game.

7. Teaches values and character.

There are many other characteristics for both situations, and the ones mentioned above are not outlandish. Most coaches are a blend of both. There is no right and wrong and, as a coach, you'll have to adjust depending on the different personalities of your players.

Head coaches all have strengths and areas that need development. I did my best to hire assistants that played at a high level, and whose personalities and areas of strength weren't the same as mine. As the head coach, you need to think in terms of how strong your coaching staff are, not just how strong you are.

In the old days, coaches said, "It's my way or the highway." That approach doesn't work anymore. Today's coaches must be willing to share the "why" behind an activity, not just say "we will" do this. Players want a coach who shows interest and concern in their efforts to improve and make them a better player. They want a coach who knows them as a person as well as a player.

I'm a big supporter of the direction our coaching associations have led us. Positive coaching is so much more rewarding and effective than the totalitarian disciplinarian coaching of the past. As coaching continues to change, I think of one of my mentors who put it best with his philosophy: "Adjust, Adapt, and Appreciate."

In my case, there would be a couple more players who would leave my program for various reasons. But I believe it is always better to stick with your philosophy and what you truly believe is best for your team. That will allow you to sleep at night. Parental decisions are not in your control, and you wouldn't want to coach a player that didn't want to be on your team anyway.

I didn't get to coach that outstanding player in high school, but when asked by another parent about it, I replied, "You can't lose what you never had."

22

How to Deal With an Upset Parent

It's not a matter of if, but when. As a coach, you *will* encounter upset parents. It is one of the most challenging aspects of our jobs.

What to do?

- Understand that, regardless of ability, their child is the most important person on earth to them.

- Accept that they will always feel the need to protect their child.

- Remind yourself that, while you may think it is, their anger is not personal. If you weren't in this position, it would be focused toward another coach.

- If they want to meet, find out why. You may need time to get any facts or thoughts together.

- Should they approach you immediately after a game, let them know you'll talk with them the next day.

- Alert your AD or Principal about any pressing issue. Don't let them hear it from someone else.

- Meet with parents as soon as possible following the brief cooling off period. Putting them off, or making them wait for an extended time, creates more tension.

- Establish guidelines at the beginning of the season for communicating with parents when they're upset:

  ✓ No emails, no texts, no posts, no voicemails

  ✓ 24 hour cooling down period

  ✓ Call the coach to set up a meeting

Have guidelines for the meeting:

✓ No other players may be mentioned or discussed.

✓ The AD or principal will attend. (Never meet alone.)

✓ Leave personal feelings and emotions at the door.

- During the meeting Listen, Listen, Listen, Listen.
  Let them get everything out before you speak. Never interrupt.
  Project positive body language and absolutely do not allow any
  distractions.

- Rather than making counter statements or arguing, you may
  want to repeat a particular statement such as, "If I understand
  you correctly, you want…" When they hear it from someone
  else, it may change or alter their view.

- Never highlight the skill deficiencies of their son or daughter. It
  serves no purpose other than to try to win the argument and
  frankly, there are no winners.

- Highlight all the positive attributes their son or daughter brings
  to the team every day. Remind them that you wouldn't have
  kept them if they weren't special.

- Review your philosophy and expectations with respect to the
  issue (such as starting, playing time, and all-tournament or
  MVP awards).

- Make no promises that can't be met. If their child isn't capable
  of starting for your team, don't say he/she is and give them false
  hope. It will come back to haunt you.

- Don't invite the parent to practice. Watching their son or
  daughter fail miserably against your best players will not help.
  Their image of them will never change, and nothing you say or
  do will alter it.

- If you made a mistake, such as failing to get a capable player in
  a game, own it. A conscientious coach would talk with the
  player or players impacted soon after the game. This would
  make the point moot by the time a meeting with the parent was
  held.

The majority of these situations revolve around playing time, starting or
not starting, and awards. Parents want their children to succeed and

often, while sitting with other parents in the stands during a game, they grow more and more angry when their child doesn't play, plays very little, or isn't the MVP. This could escalate into something ugly as the game ends if a coach hasn't discussed playing time at his or her preseason meeting. And, even then, a parent may confront you as you leave the field. The best solution at that point is to keep your composure, and just listen as they let all that anger go. Anything more, just walk away and or get your AD or security.

Doing your best at the beginning of the year to explain your philosophy with respect to starting, playing time, and awards will lay the groundwork for a great relationship with your parents. Their efforts for your program are vital to its success. However, there may be times when an upset parent contacts or approaches you; knowing why it happens, and how to deal with it in a professional way will help smooth out problems.

Section 3
Preparing Your Team

"Champions behave like champions before they are champions."
Bill Walsh

What's the key to getting your team ready to play? Can your pre-game talk win or lose the match? I think we'd all agree that practice is our laboratory for preparing our team. Those who do it best can trust their players and their decision making as the game progresses. Those who don't, tend to orchestrate every player's move. How would you rate yourself in this area?

Do you put extra effort into a pre-game speech when it's a key game? What gives your words meaning five minutes into the contest? Can your players still benefit from them? Motivation can be either uplifting or meaningless depending on the message and delivery. Most great coaches keep speeches to a minimum knowing that attention spans are low. In turn, the experience of the audience is crucial. Veteran teams know what's expected, whereas rookies may need more from you.

In this unit we shall explore the following:

- Where did you learn your motivational techniques? Would you say they're effective?

- Can you contain yourself and be brief in your speeches? Can you recognize when you've lost your team's interest?

- Do you delegate some of the pre-game preparation to your veteran leaders?

- Can you be confident that your team is prepared based on their efforts in practice?

- How will you motivate your team for that playoff spot you can't seem to secure?

23

Pregame Mental Preparation

How do you address your team before a game? Is it laced with the word 'winning'? Should it be?

In our sports-minded society, it seems winning is the only thing that's important. Players and coaches are judged on whether they win (or not) and coaches are often fired when they lose too many games. Players' abilities are often questioned when they don't win enough.

How about your team? Do you catch yourself saying, "We really need to win this game tonight!" Is winning more important to you than your players? Do they really know how important a particular game is? My guess is yes. So, with that in mind, do we overemphasize winning before the game and at halftime? By reminding players about the need to win, are we adding to the pressure and inhibiting their ability to play?

In my view, certain words and phrases add to the pressure.

1. This is a huge game.
2. Tonight is a must win.
3. Lose and we go home.
4. Everyone is counting on you.
5. Remember, no mistakes tonight.
6. We've never lost to this team.

Pointing out anything negative is never helpful before a game. In addition, emphasizing bad moments from the past can be destructive, such as:

1. Don't make the passes you did in the last game.
2. Let's play better than we did on Monday.
3. Our defending was terrible the other night.

4. Keep the ball on frame, unlike the ones in practice.

Whatever we didn't do in our previous game (or games) – this should have been taken care of at practice or discussed after the game. Negatively rehashing past moments serves no purpose now.

How can we get our point across – before the game – without overusing the word "winning?" Here are a few suggested phrases:

1. Play your best tonight.
2. Leave it all on the field.
3. Play like we practiced this week.
4. If you get tired, dig deep and believe in yourself.
5. Demand the best from each other.
6. Pick your teammates up and encourage them.
7. Let no one intimidate you. Stay focused.
8. Play with more passion than you've ever played before.
9. I am so proud of every effort you've given this season.
10. We've been here before and know what it takes to be successful.
11. You've earned the right to be here tonight.

Here's an effective mental imagery technique for doing it the right way; a means to allow your players to 'see success' before the game.

Seat the team and have them close their eyes as you set the tone with these statements and questions:

1. What do you hear?
2. Picture your teammates in a line. Walk down the line, stop, and look each one in the eye and say, "You can count on me tonight."
3. Go to your best game. What do you see? Why was it your best game?
4. Focus on the play or plays you made. How did they make you feel?
5. Think forward to this game. Picture yourself making those same plays.

6. Think how hard you've worked to get here.

7. Repeat this phrase in your mind, "Tonight is our night!"

If you do this outside the locker room before the game, your players will be able to hear the crowd which is good because it reinforces that positive mental image of support from the fans. Remind them there are many people who've supported them all year, and they're there because they believe in them.

Making players accountable to their teammates gives your athletes an extra incentive to be at their best. It reminds them the game isn't just about them; it's about the team.

Taking them back to their best game allows them to see how well they played and how capable they are of doing it again. While seeing the play is important, they also need to remember how they felt after the play and the joy and jubilation that followed.

Bringing them forward to that night's game is crucial. It reminds them of the task at hand and lets them see themselves and their teammates as having the ability to make incredible plays.

Remembering how hard they've worked throughout the season and practice justifies the right to be successful on this night.

Just saying, "Tonight is our night," will not ensure success. Players must believe in themselves and their teammates to have a chance. By being positive, offering encouragement, and laying the groundwork, you've given them a reason to believe.

We spend hours practicing technique and tactics, but it can all go up in smoke when our team isn't mentally prepared or focused. So much of that has to do with us – coaches – through our demeanor and communication. Certainly, however, no one team is like another, and preparation varies from year to year. Hopefully, by playoff time, you will have mastered the best technique to use with your team.

24

Can Your Pregame Talk Win or Lose the Game?

When your son or daughter earned their license to drive and was ready for that first solo trip, did you spend several painstaking minutes outlining every incident that might happen and what they should do? Was it for you or them? Did they look at you with confidence, knowing you had prepared them for this day: "Mom and Dad, it's okay. I'm ready to do this." Or did their body language suggest they had locked you out and weren't paying attention?

What about when, as a coach, you give your team a pregame talk? Did you spend endless minutes trying to go over every concern? Was it for you or your players? By the end, were they all paying attention, looking you in the eye? Were they engaged, or had they locked you out?

Here are a few guidelines for the pregame talk:

1. Plan - Outline what you want to cover on a card, phone, or tablet beforehand.

2. Brief - Highlight three or four major points (and each one in a sentence or less).

3. Positive - Highlight what's possible tonight, leaving negatives out.

4. Vision - Reaffirm their hard work (they earned the right to be here!).

5. Avoid meaningless information - This can run on forever.

6. Ask Questions/Get Engaged - Involve your players to keep them focused.

7. One Voice - That should be the head coach. Too much input can cloud the picture.

Ask your assistants for their input on what your major points should be before the game, and then at half time.

Most games are won or lost well after our pregame motivation techniques have worn off. Players need information that will help them in key situations, and it is such information that we need to spend time highlighting before the game and at the half. We often forget that treating our players with respect, caring about them as individuals, and involving them in team decisions truly gives them the motivation to play their best. Quality practices will cover your concerns.

What about when you see your team warming up in a casual manner and lacking focus? While this may be out of character for your team, it does happen. How and when should you act? What about unfocused behavior traveling to and from the game. How should you handle that?

We were traveling to our District Championship game facing our biggest rival. I was feeling highly tense as our starting goalkeeper was out with a broken ankle. As the ride continued, I tried to blame my uneasiness on myself as the talking and loudness of our players continued in the background. When the bus pulled up at the stadium, I was furious because I felt the players had not prepared themselves mentally for this game on the ride. As they got up, I told them to sit down. For the next three or four minutes, I let them have it and told them how upset I was. I wouldn't realize how big this mistake was until the game started. As the whistle blew, the other team played the ball wide to an outside midfielder who played a diagonal ball into space for their striker making a great run. A goal in the span of twenty seconds! Clearly my team's lack of effort and disdain for me – following my outburst – was far greater than any focus they might have had for the game. We would lose, and for the most part, it was because I mishandled the situation.

How can these situations be avoided or handled?

1. **EXPECTATIONS** - Players have to know what is expected and what will or won't be tolerated before an incident happens. A simple reminder of travel protocol, in my case, before we left the school could have alleviated this situation.

2. **TIMING** - There will be incidents that happen at key times. Understanding if they need immediate attention, or can be handled at practice or the next day, is critical.

3. **EMOTIONS** - Do your best to take your emotions out of play. Staying positive and explaining the situation from your viewpoint may be all that's needed.

4. **CONTROL** - Your control of the situation is not defined by acting at that moment. Take a moment and think things through. By controlling your reaction, you may find a solution that benefits everyone.

5. **TARGET** - We often punish the whole team for an incident that only involves one player or a small group of players. Keep the situation confined to whoever is responsible.

6. **WINNING** - As coaches, we don't have to win every battle. In trying to do so, we may lose the war as witnessed in my previous story. Ask yourself, "Is this really important, or is it so urgent that I must address it at this time?"

Coaches, like players, make mistakes over their careers. I've made my fair share of them. Often we learn best through experience, but preparation may be equally valuable in helping us to avoid situations that should never have happened. Through careful planning, players have the structure they need to act and perform to the best of their ability on and off the field. Personally, my moments of greatest frustration were when I had not clearly explained what I expected.

Take time, along with your players, to formulate a set of expectations, and remind everyone what they are every day. It will allow you to enjoy the ride to your next game and free you to concentrate on what you'll say before the game.

25
Is Your Team Ready to Play?

How many times have you coached a game against a quality opponent in which your team's play was outstanding, win or lose? What about against a weaker opponent – was your team's level of play sub-par?

As coaches, we often think that poor play is due to our players taking a weaker team for granted, but is it? Where does that thinking originate from? Certainly, some of it can begin at home with parents who plant that seed and who describe the opposition as an easy team, or maybe from classmates who do the same. But how about you as coach? Do you contribute? Let's ask ourselves the following question:

Do we plan, prepare, practice, and motivate our team for a weaker opponent with the same passion as we do for a quality opponent?

If we don't, we'll continue to be frustrated by our team's inconsistent play; inconsistent play which may cost us in a tournament. Remember, we get what we expect, and expectations start with the coach. Successful teams are able to look past all the talk and speculation and play the same way night in and night out. They only see an opponent in a different uniform and understand what their game plan is, regardless of the opposition.

It's our job as coaches to prepare our teams to the best of our abilities. I believe preparation should focus mainly on what your team does well: its strengths. You may want to tweak a few things if the opposition runs a different look than your team has seen, has one outstanding player, etc., but if you're a great defending team, get more players involved. If you're a strong attacking team, find a way to make it better. If you have a weak area on the field, exploit another area with bigger numbers. Always play to your strengths. Make the other team try to adjust.

How do you motivate your team?

I've done a host of things to motivate my teams over the years. Some have worked, and some have failed miserably. Realize that a Ra-Ra speech or gimmicks before the game will often be gone with the wind when the whistle blows. In that respect, I believe our demeanor before the game ultimately sets the tone. If players see their coach as nervous, uptight, or fidgety, they will play the same way. Do your best to have a calm demeanor during pregame warm-ups and pregame instructions.

Let the players know that this is their time to shine; it's their game and they've prepared all week for it. During practice, explain the importance of the game with every ounce of passion you have. Allow the players to absorb that thinking, shake most of their nervousness out, and then get much-needed rest before the game. The deportment of your players during a game will always be a reflection of you and what you expect.

Our players are all special and unique individuals who have different motivational drivers for playing. When we learn what those are, and build on them, our teams will be more successful. Players don't need gimmicks. They need coaches who really care about them, give 100% as they do, are always willing to help, have a desire to make them better, and are as passionate about the game as they are.

A framed picture in my office given to me by former players during an alumni game says all I need to hear about my career. **"Because of you, it's always been more than a game."**

26

Can Your Team Kick Down That Door?

Are you ready to kick that door down? You know the one I'm talking about. That team you've never been able to beat, that championship you've been chasing for years.

We were a really new team in terms of soccer years. Only five years old, but with an enthusiasm that knew no fear. Our ten seniors were the ones who had almost completely started the program as eighth graders. It was their parents who were so dedicated to getting our program going. In the next season, we would split into two high schools, so this would be our last chance. If we were going to challenge for a title, this was going to be the year. That door we were trying to kick in had footprints all over it and was creaking and moving.

In the week before our district tournament, we beat a private school in a huge upset that until then, for us, was simply unachievable. The glow on our players' faces said it all. We roared through the district tournament winning the championship 7-1. In the regional tournament, we were matched up in the first game against a team that had destroyed us 5-1 a year earlier in the same first round fixture. We talked about it but played it down, understanding that we were a different team and knowing revenge would be wasted energy. We beat them 2-1. In our next game, we defeated a young team 10-0.

As a staff, we did all we could not to embarrass or humiliate our opposition. That aspect is very important to me, because I've been on the losing side of the scoreboard before, and it's no fun. I believe we should always make sure our team isn't laughing or clowning around during those games, and we should show respect. For the regional championship game – looking us square in the eye – was a perennial powerhouse. They had already won several state championships. In the warm-up, I saw something I hadn't seen in a long time. Our players were watching the other team warm-up more than focusing on themselves. The opposition had split up into two single file lines and had jogged around both sides of the field on the touchline and around our end of the field. It had worked, we were clearly intimidated.

Our team played as hard as possible, but we lost 4-1 to an eventual undefeated state champion. The door had been slammed shut, locking us out once again. However, we would be back, having learned a valuable lesson, and would go on to become successful multiple times (albeit with a different squad). The door would eventually be opened.

As a coach how do you overcome:

1. Being defeated before the game begins?
2. Not being able to win the big game?

Are these doors closed for good or is it just a perception?

Depending on your situation, there may be factors influencing your team's ability to kick that door down:

1. Perceived unbeatable teams in your district or conference.
2. Talent pool not as strong in your school.
3. Being a really young, inexperienced team.
4. Injuries.
5. Battling your team's lack of motivation from losing to the same team year after year.
6. Divisive players influencing the team in a negative way.
7. Players with an individual agenda.
8. Parents not on board with the team's direction.

Eliminate as many of these influences as early as possible. You have control over motivating your team, teaching a young inexperienced squad, dealing with disruptive players, individualistic players, and parents to some extent. You cannot choose your district or conference, and have no control over injuries, and in public schools you have no control over the talent enrolled at your school. Only deal with, and take care of, what you can control.

The key to kicking that door down is convincing your team they can do it. I believe you can move positively toward that goal by following these steps:

1. **BE PREPARED** - Work smarter and harder in practice than any other team. Leave nothing to chance in a game situation that might derail your chances. Your players must be prepared to compete at the highest level.

2. **MOTIVATE** - Use every proven technique to motivate your team in a positive manner. Understand that too much pressure may make your team nervous, so build them up slowly.

3. **TRUST** - Do your job in practice then trust your players to make good decisions throughout the game. Let them know it's their time to shine.

4. **BE RELENTLESS** - Never give up or give in. Whether you're behind on the scoreboard, or ahead, coach to win. If you should lose, get back up and build toward the next game or next season to break through.

5. **NO EMOTION** - Play the best players all the time. This is not the time to be concerned with getting everyone in the game. Be calm in tough situations throughout the game. Your team is a reflection of you.

6. **COMPETE** - Play the toughest schedule possible throughout the year. By playing the best, you're preparing the team, young or not, for the tournament.

7. **ELIMINATE** - Either at the beginning of the year, with tryouts, or during the season if necessary, release players who are not totally committed to your program. Disgruntled players usually do their best to divide a team.

8. **BELIEVE IN YOURSELF** - When you're confident in what you're doing, the players will also be. You and your team have earned the right to be successful in this moment. Let them know.

9. **BE PASSIONATE** - Share how much this game means and what it's going to take to be successful. Showing genuine enthusiasm lets players know how serious you are.

10. **BE POSITIVE** - Players and coaches alike make mistakes during a game. Keep encouraging your players with positive statements.

11. **DEMAND THE BEST** - I love this statement, "We're better than this." It lets the players know you expect more from them, and they're capable of delivering.

12. **BUILD ON PREVIOUS DOORS** - Share all the accomplishments achieved this season and ones from previous seasons as well. Build pride in your program.

Will the above guarantee you'll kick that door down? No, but it will allow you to look in the mirror, face yourself, and know you did all that was possible on that given night to win. It will also allow you to pull yourself up and begin again with the same vigor you had to kick that door down either this year or next.

How many doors has your team kicked down? Or have you taken them for granted because of an obsession with the giant doors? In our case, some of the doors we kicked down first were:

- ✓ Defeating a private school
- ✓ Winning a District Championship
- ✓ Winning a Regional Championship
- ✓ Advancing to the Elite Eight of the State Playoffs
- ✓ Placing the first ever player on 1st Team All-State Team
- ✓ Winning 20 games in a season
- ✓ Winning a shootout
- ✓ Developing our first player to earn a college scholarship

Never forget what your team has accomplished. If you're new, ask or find out what past successes your team has achieved. Understand those successes are the foundation for you and your team to build on with everything you do. Hold them up for the team to see, and challenge them to accomplish and finish the job started by players from the beginning of the program. In your quest to kick that door down on a championship or big game, don't forget what you and the team did to get there.

27

Is Your Team Listening?

Ever look around while you're talking to your team – before the game, at practice, or during halftime – and wonder if anyone is really hearing what you're saying?

Communication issues become more evident in crucial situations at practice or during the game, or when no one seems to know how to handle matters. This can drive a coach insane, and I've lived it and witnessed it in other coaches many times.

Why do you think your team tunes you out? Possible reasons may include:

1. They're not focused on the game or practice.

2. You're not specific in what you want and who you're talking about.

3. You talk too much, and ramble.

4. You're negative, condescending, and players just turn off.

5. Your talk doesn't pertain to their position or area on the field.

6. The game may not mean that much to them.

7. They have lost respect for you.

Unfortunately, the more you contribute to this situation over time, and the more they tune you out, the less respect they'll have for everything you say. One of my mentors shared this with me: "You get what you expect."

What should we do to improve communication? And what should we expect from our players as we speak?

1. Look every player in the eye.

2. Demand they look you in the eye as well, with no crossed arms and no hands on hips.

3. Paint a positive picture of what you expect at practice and the game. Players know when they've made a mistake, no need to beat that into the ground.

4. Be specific about whose responsibility it is in a certain game/practice situation.

5. Be specific about what is breaking down/what is working.

6. Give genuine, specific praise for positives you see in the game or practice.

7. Refrain from harshly calling a specific player out in front of the team. Talk to individuals as the team breaks, or after the game or practice.

8. Don't rant and ramble. It may help you, but it means nothing to your players.

9. Keep your talk short and to the point. Require that assistants do the same.

10. Ask players to repeat what was just mentioned.

11. Embolden your players to ask questions and speak up, then listen to their viewpoints.

12. Never follow one of their statements with a throw-away statement, such as "Yes, but..." or "Good idea."
"Good idea" without specifics, has little meaning.

13. Remember, players want to play.

We all want our players to respect us. It doesn't come automatically with the title of coach, however. We have to earn it, just as they have to earn it with us. When we respect players as individuals and as part of a team, it will build their respect for us. Listening works both ways. By reaffirming and modeling positive listening habits with our team, we show them how important it is.

Communication in all forms is a key component of building a team and a program.

It's a team game, and we all need each other. Paying attention to the small details and how we treat our players will give us all a greater chance for success.

28

Is Your Team Ready for a Tournament Run?

As tournament time draws near, questions and concerns arise. Is your team prepared to make a championship run? What are the essentials in preparation? Are there particular roadblocks to avoid during the season? Is there one area that's more important than any other?

Have you thought things out during the season? Calculated in your mind how every practice was a building block for your tournament run? Covered every situation possible? Sharpened your team's technique? Put the players in challenging situations to strengthen their mental toughness?

What about your schedule? Did you ever think it may be the most important part of your preparation for the tournament and subsequent success?

The makeup and talent of your team should determine every aspect of your thinking as you make your schedule.

1. **VETERAN SQUAD** - Challenging them throughout the season is a must! Schedule teams of equal or greater talent. The key is spacing games out. Start with an opening game against one of the power teams, teams that are top five, or last year's champion. This will gauge your team's ability, let them know where they stand, and how they need to improve. Play a couple more top teams during the middle of the season, preferably in a tournament atmosphere, and then schedule one top match the week before the last week of the season. You want your players to be able to recover from a win or loss, mentally and physically, before the tournament begins. If you play a high-profile rival, play them toward the middle of the year; those games can really drain your team. If possible enter another tournament (i.e. a total of two) during the season. A tournament atmosphere cannot be duplicated in a regular season game. Playing the majority of your games on the road is another great

way to prepare your veteran team. Many of the state tournament games will be away from home in hostile environments, so get your players ready.

Don't be distracted by polls/ranking and where you stand. This team knows what they want to accomplish. Stay away from soft opponents and the majority of home games. There are no soft teams in championship games.

2. **YOUNG TEAM** - Some coaches attempt to bring a young team on by starting out with very soft teams to gain wins. They'll schedule other soft teams throughout the season to build confidence and gain more wins. The result can be a young team with a 15-2 record that is eliminated in the first game of district play by a ridiculous scoreline. While on paper the record looks impressive, the tournament results beg to differ. There is a balance to be had in this situation. It's important that your team wins some games to gain confidence; however, you need to challenge them at different points in the season. Scheduling half the games on the road and half at home is a good idea when possible. Games on the road are – more often than not – tougher than playing at home. Also, balance your schedule out with several teams that are of equal or better talent. Young teams must learn and experience what it's like to play against teams where every aspect of their training comes into play. Otherwise, you and your team have no idea how you've progressed or what you need to work on.

Stay away from wins/losses as an indicator of your success. This may be a rebuilding/growing year where meaningful progress will only be measured in the coming seasons.

3. **A BLEND OF YOUTH AND VETERANS** - More often than not, this will be the makeup of your team. Scheduling will really hinge on the talent level of your team rather than players' tenure. Certainly, there will be no need to bring this team along slowly unless the veterans are few in number and the young players dominate the scene. Put together a strong schedule with two or three top ten teams. Space them evenly throughout the year, and enter your team in a tournament or two to give them valuable experience. Play the majority of your games on the road and schedule your rival twice – in a home and away scenario – if possible. As you schedule games, other than top ten competitors, make sure you play teams in your region that you might play in the tournament. It will give you insight on

how you match up with those teams. Playing a soft team 80 miles away that you will never see in the tournament is pointless. Should they call, never shy away from a tough opponent.

Soft opponents should be avoided with this team. They only give your team a false image of how good they are. This team needs to develop a mental toughness of what it takes to be successful. While having a winning season may be important, the only thing they will remember is how well they did in the tournament.

Everything about your scheduling should build on preparing your team for the postseason. Only you know your team with respect to talent and makeup. Challenging them with tough opponents in tough situations will teach you more about their ability, toughness, and character than any other situation. Players want to be challenged. They want to improve. Do your best by giving them a schedule that provides that environment. Ask more from your team than they think is possible, and your team will be better for it.

29

Does Your Team Have Hope?

Hope. Such a powerful word.

We all hear inspiring stories of individuals overcoming insurmountable odds because they, or those around them, had hope. It's that strand we can all hang onto even in the darkest of times. But where does hope come from?

Often we hear that hope is possible through faith in a higher power, ourselves, and those around us. Amazingly it's not something we can see, feel or touch, but for those of us who know how to summon it when needed, it's as visible as the shining sun. It wraps its arms around us, and we can almost reach out and touch it.

What about your team? Do they have hope as the season begins? What does that hope encompass? A winning season, no injuries, a championship? Coaches often put little credence in hope. They would say that hoping for a championship won't win it; hoping is not enough. Hard work and action are what wins titles.

I would agree that just sitting around hoping to win will not help you win games. But what if we add hope to our practices, pregame talks, and beyond… every chance we get? Changing the mental framework of our team can provide hope in a tough game. We must give our team the ability to rise up and accomplish the seemingly impossible. It's only possible if hope is present, and players believe they can do it.

Can "hope" influence the outcome of your game or program? Have you ever caught yourself thinking, "I hope we play well tonight," or "I hope he or she is on their game." Is hope a word we need to avoid or lose as a coach so that we only focus on tangible attributes that influence our game?

Think back to when you played. Were there games in which there was almost no hope of your team winning? Were there seasons where hope was non-existent due to inexperience or injuries? Do highly successful teams rely on hope? I believe they do, even if it's indirect. How can we instill hope in our players, especially if they're struggling for success?

Here a few ways to foster hope and faith in your team:

1. **ENCOURAGE** - Can you remember how much hope you gained when a coach encouraged you? It made you work harder and believe in yourself, giving you confidence. Take the time to do that every day with your players

2. **SETBACKS** - There will be plenty. Use them as building blocks for your team. Setbacks – whether individual (injury) or team (loss) – can dim our hopeful outlook, but how long that dimness lasts is up to the coach. Learn, move on, and build your team back up.

3. **FOCUS** - Hope can take a big hit when we get caught up in everything about our opponent. Don't overwhelm your team with everything the other team does well or what you must stop. Focus on what your team does well and how it's going to give the other team problems. Our team has worked hard, and they deserve to be in this position. Let them know how much you believe in them.

4. **CHALLENGE/PREPARE** - For your team to have hope, most players need to see proof. Put them in tough situations in practice (numbers down, way down) and let them dig their way out. If they can't, make them do it again until they can. When they do, let them know this is what it's going to take to be successful, and that they did it.

5. **BELIEVE** - Hope is made stronger when an individual or team knows their leader really believes they can accomplish anything. It has to be genuine. They also have to believe in themselves and their teammates. Take time to stop practice when you see a player or players being successful. Paint the picture, replay the situation, and reaffirm the outcome.

6. **EMPOWER** - It's almost impossible to lead the team by yourself solely. The team needs one or more leaders on the field. They must be willing to be tough and demanding with little regard for feelings and more concerned with everyone doing their job. Without true leaders, your team will never reach its potential. Teach and support them in molding your team. Your true appreciation for them will be more apparent when they've graduated.

7. **INSPIRATION** - Whether it's guest speakers who've beaten the odds in terrible situations, video clips, or personal stories from you or other team members, drive home the point that when you have hope you have everything you need. Take the time to talk about hope, what it is, where it comes from, and why some people seem to have it more than others.

I'm sure you can remember a game where a team just kept coming at you, even when your skill and strength outmatched them. You had to marvel at their relentless spirit. They had hope, and when a team has it, they can accomplish anything. I was part of such an experience and proud to say it was our team:

It was the biggest comeback I had ever been a part of...

We were trailing 3-0 at the half. As the second half played down, we scored one, then two goals to tighten things up. You could see the hope and confidence building in our players as they started encouraging each other. Heart, desire, and determination driven by hope were evident in everything we did.

Two minutes were left, and we still trailed. We just couldn't get another one in the back of the net. I had almost come to the realization that we wouldn't win but felt proud of how we had fought back in this half. Suddenly, with 30 seconds left, our midfielder won the ball at the top of the 18 and headed towards the goal. She was amazing, beating one of their strikers and two midfielders, powering across the halfway line. The opposition had two very skilled defenders who weren't about to let her score. They angled her away from the goal.

At that moment almost everyone thought we were done, but not her. She headed straight for the end line and looking back saw one of her teammates racing unmarked into the penalty box. As she got to the end line, she played a perfect back angle ball on the ground across and away from the six-yard box and the goalkeeper. It went directly to her teammate who simply ran onto the ball and placed it in the corner of the goal as the horn sounded. I'll never forget what we had accomplished and the celebration that followed. Coming back from a three-goal deficit is almost unheard of in our game. We went on to win the game in a shootout.

I believe "hope" is a combination of what we have, such as the skills and strategy learned in practice, experience learned in other games, and faith in ourselves and our teammates. These all nurture hope and free us to have a vision of success.

Hope comes with a vision. Regardless of the situation we're in, initially we have a vision of a positive outcome. That vision is based on our faith and experience, and our belief in those who care about us. Once that vision is lost, so is hope. On a smaller scale, your team needs to see that vision. Share it every day with your team, and know – as long as you're there – the vision of hope will continue to shine.

30
Motivation: Real or Contrived?

Have you ever attended a seminar or clinic where the speaker was spellbinding, and you absorbed every word? Did you want to run out and apply every principle they outlined? Was it because of who the speaker was? Their charisma? The content? What they had accomplished using the principles they advocated?

I'll guess you've had such an experience and you were motivated by it. But for how long?

What motivates you? Does it play a part in how you motivate your team? Does it impact upon your ability to motivate your team effectively? There are certain topics, activities, and concepts we feel comfortable with, allowing us to convey our message in a sincere way. Conversely, other motivational techniques may not feel right with us.

Every coach has searched for that magic formula to propel their team to success. But does a magic formula actually exist? Contrary to conventional wisdom, I believe it does. The secret is realizing it exists in many forms and shapes for different teams and different circumstances.

How many of you have tried something to motivate your team, and it failed miserably? How did you know? Was it because you lost the game? Maybe it worked, and the score was closer than if you had used nothing. Did you ever think a lesson learned might be more important than a win? Motivation is hard to measure, and that measurement is often in wins and losses.

Finding the right motivation at the right time...

This was the big night. The tension was everywhere. We had advanced to the state playoffs, and a trip to the final four was on the line. The day before, I had stayed on the field after practice and spent a couple of hours sitting on our bench thinking of the best way to motivate our team.

I played the game in my mind as I sat there and wondered what it would take to give our team the edge. Too much motivation would make us nervous early in the game and might work against us, too little and we'd be flat and vulnerable to giving up a goal.

Finally, after arriving home feeling overwhelmed with too many ideas, my phone rang. It was Janie. She had played on one of our previous regional championship teams but then moved away. She wanted to wish us the best of luck and was sorry she couldn't be there to cheer us on. You could sense the sincerity in her voice.

After telling her we'd have our hands full and the challenges we faced, she came up with an idea that was truly wonderful. She reminded me of a tradition we had of giving jerseys to former players after a few years if they wanted them, and said she wanted me to cut her shirt up and give a piece to each player to put in their socks for the game.

If she couldn't be there, she wanted a former champion's spirit riding with the players during the game. "Wow!" was all I could say. I had no problem relaying her message in a heartfelt way to our team before the game. As I cut the jersey in front of our players and handed the pieces out, I could see by their expressions that motivation need not be loud and theatric. The connection to another champion and her willingness to make a sacrifice for players she didn't know was felt by everyone. Nothing else had to be said.

On that night we were defeated by a better team, but the motivation given to us by Janie would allow us to play the best game of the year. Clearly, the lesson learned from her willingness to give was more important than the game.

I believe there are several ingredients that have to be in place for motivation to be effective.

Key ingredients for successful motivation

1. **REAL/SINCERE** - Is it real and sincere? Players know when your efforts are sincere. Do you really believe in your message and what you're asking the players to do? Is it just some theatrical performance or gimmick to get the team pumped up? Theatrics or trashing the other team before the game usually only last for a couple of minutes and then the highly skilled team takes over. Let your players know how proud you are to be their coach.

2. **BENEFITS** - What's in it for the team? It can't be just for you. Do they really want to achieve the championship or win on this

night? Remind them of all they've done to prepare for this game. They play the game, so build the value for them.

3. **CREDIBLE** - Motivation can be overdone. If you've shredded the other team's jersey, torn up press clippings, etc. before every game – your act is probably getting old with the team. Save the true motivation for key games when the team understands you really mean it, and it's not another act.

4. **THREATENING OR REWARDING** - Negative motivation can work against a team. Making them fearful of losing the contest rarely works out. A scared team usually plays scared. Use your motivation to explain the rewards that come with playing a great game.

5. **AUDIENCE** - When you motivate your team, are you reaching them all? Probably not, but are you reaching the key players? Every player is motivated in different ways, so make sure your leaders understand your message. Their ability to convey that message in words and actions to the rest of the team will make the difference.

6. **WORTH IT** - Paint a picture for your team when motivating them. Some have never been where you believe your team is capable of going. It has to be worth the effort and commitment for your motivation to work. A former or current player speaking before the game can paint the picture you need.

Rah-Rah motivation before a game usually lasts for a few minutes, and then skill level and preparation take over. Don't spend too much time on some far-out motivational technique or theatrics to pump your team up. Great teams know what they need to do to be successful.

Spend time on quality motivation. Explain to your team:

1. The sacrifice and commitment they've put in to get here.

2. How proud you are to be their coach.

3. Their accomplishments to this point.

4. Who they represent.

5. What they are capable of.

6. How much they mean to each other.

7. Moments like this are once in a lifetime.

8. How much confidence you have in them.

9. Those who have worn the jersey they currently wear.

10. Never be satisfied with where you are, only where you're going.

The best time to motivate your team is during and after practice on the day before the game. Remind your players of the goals the team set for the season, the individual goals they set for themselves, and the importance of this game. By doing so, you remind them of the motivation necessary to be successful.

31

Heart, Desire, and Determination

Have you ever won a game you weren't supposed to win? Not necessarily an upset, but a game where – from a skill standpoint – your team wasn't on par with your competitor. What allowed you to escape with a win? Was it a new strategy you put in just for that game? Replacing a player? A lucky goal?

There are times when we feel we made a key decision or move that got us the win, but could it have had more to do with our players' Heart, Desire, and Determination than anything else? Where does that come from? Is it something a player is born with, or is it developed over time? Can it be taught?

I believe there are key ingredients that create an atmosphere for Heart, Desire, and Determination to grow and develop for players and teams. With those ingredients in place, especially in games where you're matched up against teams of similar or somewhat greater skill, you will have a greater chance of success.

It was the biggest win our school had experienced in a while...

We were playing in our district tournament with the winner moving on to regionals. Our school hadn't made it out of the district in six years, and this wasn't going to be easy. In our two previous matches, we'd ended in a tie, and settled nothing in overtime. Moving on to penalty kicks we had been defeated both times. That image did not escape me as the game began, and I wondered if our players felt the same way.

Why would anyone expect anything different tonight? You could see the determination on our players' faces, especially our seniors. We had taken the lead, 1-0, only to see the opposition tie it in the second half.

On a corner kick, towards the end of the second half, we played a beautiful head-high ball to the back post where one of the team was positioned perfectly as she headed it in. For the next eight minutes, our rivals attacked relentlessly. They even had a corner kick, right as the clock ticked down to zero, which came close.

Several of our players collapsed to the ground, literally physically and mentally exhausted from the burden and weight of this game. I was so proud of what they had accomplished and knew they had poured everything into the game.

What are the ingredients necessary for Heart, Desire, and Determination?

1. **BELIEVE IN THEIR COACH** - Players who believe in their coach will play harder than they thought possible. Developing a trusting and caring atmosphere for your players lays the groundwork to ask for more effort when needed. Players know whether you have their best interests at heart.

2. **FEARLESS** - With no fear of being ridiculed by the coach, players will take on challenges with a positive attitude, knowing they can accomplish anything. And often they do. Fearless players win games for your team.

3. **BELIEVE IN THEMSELVES** - As coaches begin to believe in their players, something magical happens: players start to believe in themselves. It sounds so simple, but quite often never happens because players sense the coach doesn't trust their abilities or decisions. Build your players up every chance you get.

4. **RELENTLESS** - Players who believe in themselves have superhuman qualities that allow them never to accept being tired, being beaten, or thinking in negative terms concerning the outcome of a game. They know they can be successful one more time throughout the game and never quit.

5. **POSITIVE VISION** - While others around them worry about the status of a top opponent, these players just look at it as an opportunity to do something special against a quality side. Their thoughts never wander to a place that lets them believe there's no way they can win. They only see a vision of victory.

6. **BELIEVE IN THEIR TEAMMATES** - These players have a never-ending belief in their teammates and what they can all do

to succeed. They spend time encouraging and motivating their teammates in an effort to show them how much they really believe in their abilities. An unbreakable bond is developed, tying the team together, allowing them to do seemingly impossible tasks.

7. **MODELED BY THE COACH** - It's easy to forget our responsibility to be everything we want our players to be, even when we expect it from our players. Genuinely care about your players, encourage them at every chance you get, push them to improve, trust their abilities and decision making, and put them in a position to be successful. Take the blame in losses and give them the credit in victories. Protect and always stand up for your players, and show them that *your* Heart, Desire, and Determination is just as strong as theirs.

How can you measure Heart, Desire, and Determination? Are there any tests that will give you data to know your players have it (or that certain players have it more than others)? I don't think so. Heart, Desire, and Determination are somewhat like the wind. You can feel it, see its impact, and quite often hear it, but it's hard to see. And so it is with your players. You can see their skills quite easily, but it's hard to see if – deep down – they have that true Heart, Desire, and Determination it takes when the game is on the line.

When you provide a positive environment for those ingredients to grow, you'll see an immediate impact with your team. A team that believes in themselves, their coach, and their teammates, approaches a game in a fearless manner and is relentless in their efforts. That's an advantage you can't afford to be without.

Section 4
Look in the Mirror

"Shout praise and whisper criticism." Don Meyer

Where do you turn in times of crisis? Do you criticize others? Do you take the blame? Even if it's clearly a player's fault, we need to absorb some (or all) of the blame. Incidents where players made a mistake can have a devastating impact on their lives. It costs us nothing to shoulder the blame to the media or anyone else who wants an explanation.

What about after a loss? Do we run our players into the ground the next day at practice? I believe we need to look in the mirror after any incident and ask if we could have done something better. We're the leaders and ultimately responsible for everything on our team. On the flip side, we should always give our players credit when they're successful. It doesn't matter that we called the play or put them in a position to make the play. They get the credit! Our reward is that feeling we get when we see them happy.

In this unit we will share the following:

- Have you ever blasted a team after a loss, only to realize they've blasted themselves long before you spoke?

- Do you look in the mirror after a loss and ask yourself tough questions?

- Is there someone who can give you an honest assessment of you and your team?

- Are you able to see yourself like your players see you?

- Can you be gracious in defeat and humble in success?

32

Are You an Inspiration?

Coaches and athletic programs conduct research and invest a lot of time and money to find motivation and techniques that work. So what is the best method of motivating your team? What's the key to being the spark?

Experience tells us that if we can motivate our team to play their absolute best, they'll be successful. It's a never-ending task coming up with new ideas, refining old ones, delivering speeches, video clips, innovative activities and strategies to keep your team engaged. How can we be sure of their impact?

First, we should ask what the essence of motivation is. Pretty simple really: it's inspiration. Can you inspire your team to play better than they've ever played before?

Often coaches rely on their background and playing experience at a high level to carry them through; telling stories about their playing days and accomplishments. I've known successful coaches who played at a high level and those who barely played. Honestly, most young players could not care less where you played, how many championships you won, and the superstars you hung out with. They're mainly concerned with their game and their lives. That may sound like a negative, but when you recognize it as one of your biggest challenges, you're on your way to finding out what works best for your team.

If you played at a high level, you've experienced outstanding practices and game situations that will guide you at key times, but you will need so much more than that.

Being an inspiration has more to do with who you are than where you played.

Inspiration involves being:

1. **CREDIBLE** - Credibility is earned over time. Everything you say and do is being watched and evaluated by your players. Remember to be consistent in your decisions, and always put

the team first. Credibility, like respect, takes time to earn but can be lost in an instant.

2. **GENUINE** - There's no need to act like or be anyone else. We all have strengths and weaknesses. Continue to work on areas you feel need attention, but build and use your strengths to the team's advantage. As an example, if you're a humble coach, don't try to hide it, use it as a positive example for your team. If you're a demanding coach, use it to challenge your players in a non-threatening way.

3. **CARING** - There will be situations, such as a family tragedy or season-ending injury, where you need to step up and be there for your player or players. If it means canceling practice or a game, or you being away from the rest of the team, do it. Your ability to care during these tough times will be more important than any game your team has ever played. Our game is just that, a game. This is life.

4. **HUMBLE** - Be a great example of humility for your team. Let your players rejoice in their triumphs while you're in the background. Keep in mind that this is their time to shine. Remind the team after a big win how to conduct themselves, knowing how it feels to lose as well.

5. **HONEST** - When you make decisions, never rush them. Weigh up all the options and be honest with your players. Always tell them the truth, even when it isn't easy. Speaking the truth is something you will never look back on with regret.

6. **CHALLENGING** - Challenging your players every day will earn their respect. Never allow them to settle for yesterday's accomplishments. Players will never come back and complain about being challenged. Inspire them to improve through your persistence and high standards.

7. **OF STRONG CHARACTER** - Over the years I've probably used this phrase more than any other, "Remember you represent your school, your family, and your team." We need to realize it applies to us as well, whether we're with our team or out in the community. Our actions will always be on display as a "coach", not just an ordinary individual. Keep in mind that we're held to a higher standard, and we should act accordingly.

When you address your team before a game, do you truly believe your message? If not, don't say it. Do you believe in them? They get messages every day concerning mistakes they've made in games, or that they need to work harder from family and friends. They need you to believe in their ability to succeed, and for you to say it. When they know it, they can and will do amazing things in the game.

The greatest compliment a player can give a coach is, "He/She believed in me."

Your credibility with your team will be the deciding factor on how well you can motivate them. Does this guarantee you will win a title or titles? Certainly not! It does guarantee that your team will give their most consistent effort night in and night out because they believe that what you say is true. They know through your examples and actions that you have their best interests at heart.

Once you've earned their trust, there's no need for gimmicks or techniques that only last for a few minutes. The game is much longer than that. Your team needs substance, inner strength, and a solid foundation of beliefs to persevere to the final horn. What you've established is the answer to the question, "What is most effective in motivating my team?" and will have far more impact than anything else.

The inspiration is you.

33

What Image Are You Projecting?

We expect a lot from our players in everything they do, whether it's on the field or off it. Paramount is our expectation that they will be fit and healthy.

While for most of us, our playing days may be over, many of us have been athletes or involved in fitness of some type in the past. We know from experience what it means to embody the image of health.

What image are you portraying as you talk to your players today? What do your players see as the words about fitness, dedication, and commitment come pouring out of your mouth? Are you a positive model for them in your appearance and actions? Are you fit? Do you dress professionally at practice and at games?

Should they take you seriously if your example is the complete opposite of what you're saying?

You might argue that it's not what you look like but what you know, and I'd agree with you to a point. Your knowledge and ability to convince your team as to what you are saying is more important than how you look. But do you really have their complete respect? I'm not talking about being able to run a mile in five minutes, play 90 minutes, or sprint like you did in high school or college.

I'm talking about being fit with respect to your stage of life. Are you able to take part in an activity with your team if needed, or if you feel like it? Can you do conditioning exercises with them? Let's remember, modeling behavior with respect to fitness and nutrition is our responsibility.

Looking at it from a selfish standpoint, your fitness is more important than ever. Without being fit and extending your life, the knowledge you have will be lost. What an unnecessary waste that would be! The excellent facilities available to most of us allow us to stay in shape by working out before or after practice, or with our teams.

As we all know, a fitness routine is only half the puzzle. Our nutrition plays a big role in our total fitness, quality of life and longevity. Do you spend any time with your team talking about or bringing in an expert with respect to nutrition? If you coach a girls' team, it's especially important with the threat of anorexia and bulimia present. But those aren't just confined to girls' teams; boys suffer from these conditions as well.

Players also need to know the risks and potential dangers of supplements, and certainly the long term effects of steroids and bodybuilding and shaping drugs. Cumulative risks often don't grab the attention of a young player who has no immediate symptoms of an illness or disease. Your players need to be aware of the risks, and we can't take for granted that someone else is teaching them.

As an example of how nutrition-conscious players are more inclined to do what's right, my team came to me and said, "We don't want to stop at the regular burger place. We want to stop at the sandwich place without all the fat and calories." I thought it was great! I must admit, this is an area that I didn't focus a lot on with my team. I feel certain that most of us are concerned with technique, tactics, conditioning, and team building more than spending time on nutrition.

Rather than becoming an expert on the subject, ask someone from your school, someone from the health department, or a nutrition expert from your area to talk with the team. Even if you give up one day of practice every year, your players will hear a message they might not normally hear. All you have to do is look around at our society to see the urgent need for this education.

As coaches, we have to walk the walk and be an example to our team. If your fitness and nutritional practices aren't what they should be, start to make a change today. Be up front with your team and let them know the path you are on. They will be more than glad to help you. It will bring you and your team closer together, and I know it will help them with their own challenges. Even if you are not as successful as you'd like to be, they will see you care.

While your players may not play into old age, fitness and nutrition will always be a big part of their adult lives and play a huge role in family life. Our job extends a lot farther than the field or court.

As far as looking professional, think of it this way: if you want to be taken seriously, *look like it*. The mirror will never lie. Your players want to be proud to call you their coach. You'll never get a chance to change that first impression, so make it a good one. Your players, and many others, are watching.

34
Who Are You?

Most of us can answer this with a degree of certainty. As you think about the question, you begin to recall moments in your career that define who you are. The ones that come to mind first are usually the highlight reels from successful times, and then those moments we'd like to forget creep into our consciousness – decisions we'd like to change.

I've heard coaches say, "I never look back on decisions I've made." While I agree there is little you can do to change the outcome, you *can* look back and learn. So I ask the question again, "Who are you?"

What really drives your coaching career? Is it all about winning? Are you pursuing a championship? Is it the notoriety? Are you attempting to break some coaching records? Are you just in it for the money? Who would you be today if you just walked away from coaching? After all, isn't that *who* you really are? A unique individual buried beneath all the many layers of coaching.

Many coaches are defined by their obsession with winning. Their ability to relate to their players is restricted to a business-like approach of 'I'm the coach so do what I say.' They preach a sermon of sacrifice, hard work, and toughness. Many win a lot of games, but at what cost?

Often they're overly harsh with their players, criticizing everything they do in front of the team, and never really taking the time to get to know them. I might add they do 'care' about their players, but it's an old-school caring of tough love without the ability to construct a strong relationship built on trust and respect. This style of coaching – while the norm years ago – simply doesn't work for the majority of players today, often turning them away from your team or the sport altogether.

Your coaching metal will be forged...

Our coaching careers were all shaped at an early age by our youth coaches. Have you ever taken a moment to think about your former coaches and how similar, or in some cases so directly opposite, your style is?

In my case, my coach (who I admired) was an extremely tough disciplinarian, often going over the top in verbally abusing players. I vowed that if I ever coached, I'd never talk to or treat players the way he did. Throughout a 20 year career I was told over and over again that I wasn't tough enough to coach. Those who said this didn't know who I was, or where I had come from. I always found their criticisms a compliment.

Old school traditions and coaching practices still linger in the minds of parents who also had these types of coaches. Sadly, I have had parents tell me to be tougher on their kids. My metal was still being shaped.

...and shaped.

How about you? Are you obsessed with winning a championship? I know throughout my career that was always one of my goals, but I didn't think it defined who I was. I once cut a player who had a disability. As I look back now, *how could I do that*? She would have played on our JV team and been an inspiration to the rest of our players. My vision was clouded, then, by what I thought a player should be able to do, with little thought to how I could impact a life. All I could see was a championship.

Some of the Ingredients that shape our coaching metal are:

1. Our Youth Coaches.
2. Our Parents.
3. Our Players/Their Parents.
4. Mentors/Heroes.
5. Our Faith.
6. Circumstances.
7. Rules/Regulations.
8. Past Experiences.
9. Expectations.
10. Our Wider Family.
11. Our Values/Integrity.

None of us are the same; we have varying degrees of each ingredient. What makes us unique are:

1. Our Reactions.
2. Our Heart.

I believe Reactions and Heart define who you are as a coach more than anything else. While initially appearing to be opposites, they're very similar. They can be outwardly visible, and just as easily be unseen. In both scenarios, they still have a huge impact on players.

Reactions to mistakes, successes, and every situation in between, say a lot about who you are as a coach. Is our reaction over the top, is it appropriate or not? Does it help the situation or inflame it? Have we considered all the facts? Should we react immediately or wait for a better time? Is our reaction positive or negative?

We all know how explosive coaches react to different situations, and we're also in awe of coaches who seem never to react outwardly to tough situations. Where would you say you fit on that spectrum?

With respect to our Heart, do our players know we genuinely care about them as an individual and not just as a player? Do we take the time to make sure they're doing well in the classroom? Do we ask about their family? Do we know what their other talents are, and what career they're interested in pursuing? Can you show compassion during a tough time in their lives? Could you put aside their sports careers and recommend they devote more time to their family or another situation that needs them?

In the old days, motivation was based on fear. Players did what the coach said because they didn't want to be punished. Today, motivation is built on trust and respect. That trust and respect is formed by coaches with Heart who care about their players in a genuine way. Are you a caring coach?

Take the time today to think about your situation and who you are as a coach. What worked in the old days won't work today. Can you still show toughness and guide players to new levels of success? Absolutely! The difference is the vehicle required to get them there. Coaches who understand this message are the ones who will be successful and impact their players the most.

35

Is the Program About You?

I frequently hear coaches – at every level – preaching the phrase, "It's not about me; it's about my players." I'm not sure who they're trying to convince… themselves or everyone else? Many coaches seem to hide behind that phrase when everyone who's familiar with their program knows differently. It is about them and always will be.

Is that bad? It can be bad if a coach's ego always gets in the way of making decisions in the players' interests. It's as if the coach is always stepping in front of the players to rob them of the spotlight. Those coaches' first question to themselves in challenging times is always: "How will this impact me?"

Let's explore the supposedly selfish statement: "It is about me." When you think about it in a positive way, everything your team is and becomes **is about you**. It's knowing and dealing with the power and responsibility that comes with that concept that's essential.

I understand the need to protect players with respect to the media, and to take the blame for a loss or other negative issues. Throughout my career, I always did my best to stay in the background and let my players get credit for and enjoy their successes. However, we have to accept responsibility for everything that happens and know that, in this respect, our program is *about us*.

Players and parents pass through year after year, but if we're fortunate enough to stay with the same program, we are the one constant and everything it represents is a reflection of us. We should never take that lightly, or be consumed by the power that comes with it. The challenge is finding a balance between what we feel is best for our team and our willingness to be out in front.

When do coaches need to be in the spotlight?

1. After a loss.

2. When there are issues or challenges.

3. When highlighting or talking about our players.

4. When selling our program or plans for the future.

5. At media events for coaches.

Many coaches become absorbed with their programs and ultimately embarrass themselves and their institutions when they refuse to leave, or when they publicly ridicule or undermine their bosses. Sadly, they feel the program is **only** about them. In these cases, the power of the position, not their players, has become their focus. I would agree that they built the program into a success, but somewhere along the line, they lost track of their priorities. We have to remember the program should always be about the organization, the players, and the coach, in that order.

How can coaches avoid the ego trap?

1. Keep success in perspective; it can be fleeting.

2. Be humble; remember your roots.

3. Put the players' interests first in everything you do.

4. Revisit your priorities every year.

5. Have a mentor and assistants who can question what you're doing.

6. Ask yourself, "Is this for the players or me?"

When we truly embrace humility and understand our role in building and developing a program, we can constantly realize our responsibilities. While the program is about us, there is no need to use that power for anything other than the betterment of our players and the organization they are part of.

36

Can You Handle the Truth?

Can you step back and see yourself as your players do? As a player, what personality traits of yours would draw *you* in? What traits would push *you* away?

It's really tough to be fair with these questions because you're naturally biased. As coaches, we see ourselves in a different light; many coaches see themselves as calculated and tough, keeping a distance from their players, and only dealing with making them better players. While others lean to the other side, saying the game itself isn't as important as the life lessons taught and the caring atmosphere provided.

Is either side right or wrong? Not really, but there's no way to truly evaluate our impact and the climate of our team without outside help. Who steers us back on course during the season when we wander off and things aren't going well? Who can get in our ear and honestly tell us what we need to do? Will we listen? We often think we have all the answers, but we need help just like our players.

I believe coaches stubbornly wait until it's almost too late (and in some cases it is) before they seek assistance. So where should we turn?

- **ASSISTANT COACHES** - can give you feedback or make suggestions on your performance, but often they've grown close, or may be reluctant to offer criticism because they are concerned about their jobs. Hiring Assistant Coaches who aren't afraid to give their opinions and ideas is a must. Look for coaches who aren't the mirror image of yourself with respect to personality and demeanor. You don't need someone to agree with everything you say and do.

- **MENTORS** - Every one of us either learned from or admired another coach as we began our career. How about contacting that coach, and asking what they would do in the same situation? Often they have a great solution, and in some cases, it spurs fresh thinking on how best to solve the problem (or it reaffirms you're on the right path). It's never a sign of weakness to do what's best for you and your team and ask for help.

- **ATHLETIC DIRECTOR** - Your Athletic Director is usually a former coach, and a great resource to lean on. Most ADs know what it's like to be mired in the trenches of coaching. Some coaches are reluctant to share issues and problems with their AD because they see it as a sign of weakness which could impact their employment. Another drawback is that he or she isn't around every day, so it's impossible for them to evaluate you adequately on seeing your team play a few games, your win-loss record, and complaints/compliments from players' parents.

- **PLAYERS** - Assistant Coaches, Mentors, and ADs are good ideas but how can we gauge who we really are as a coach, our effectiveness, and our impact on our team? The answer is right in front of you. Yes… your team. When you consider who knows you the best, *it's your team.*

Asking your players may be the best solution.

If you're willing to hear the truth right now, have a team meeting. I recommend setting ground rules for the meeting to keep it civil and focused. Write any characteristics, or areas you wish to be evaluated on, across a smart board or easel and talk about them one by one while everyone is present. By talking about your evaluation, other issues about the team will ultimately surface.

Some will be about you, and others will be about the team. Keep the meeting on track concerning your performance and then come back to the other issues. The key will be filtering through issues that have little impact on your team and which are just individual gripes. Be ready for the way they're presented, and the emotions. I don't recommend a handout; it is a mistake to ask all the players to evaluate you and also write issues down while they're in the same room.

When planning the meeting, you may want to involve your team leaders or veterans because, at some levels, younger players may or may not understand the purpose of the exercise and be unwilling or unable to contribute. On the plus side, younger players gain insight into what you expect and how you handle situations. You may also want to meet with your team leaders before the meeting so they can be aware of what to expect and formulate ideas ahead of time.

Three team dynamics may be present at a team meeting:

1. **TRUST** - Your team trusts you as a coach, as well as their teammates. They feel comfortable giving you and each other an

honest appraisal without retribution. This is usually a veteran team with strong leadership. Sharing concerns is done in a mature manner while establishing solutions.

2. **DISSENSION** - Your team is in disarray, and action needs to be taken. These meetings can get ugly and feelings will get hurt, but often they're necessary. Moderate them so no player is persecuted by all the players, and establish guidelines for remarks. Be ready for the team to give you suggestions on how you can improve.

3. **COMBINATION** - This is usually the most common. You'll have a few of your players who want to dominate the meeting and air issues, with the rest being compliant and saying very little. You will have to dig a little deeper with this team to make sure everyone is heard.

You spend most of your time with your players during practice, traveling, and games. *They're the most qualified people to evaluate your coaching impact.* Are they qualified to assess your abilities with respect to game situations, tactics, and strategy? Usually not, but don't underestimate their intuition with respect to how you care for them, how team chemistry operates, and the overall climate of the squad.

Ignoring or hoping that the climate of your team will take care of itself rarely happens, and when it does it's probably not the way you wanted. We can learn a lot from our players by allowing them to voice their opinions and be heard. Take time to listen to their ideas genuinely and show an interest in their lives. The rewards will last a lifetime.

37

Are You Costing Your Team?

How would you describe your demeanor? Calm, excitable, angry, stoic? What about in tough situations when you feel your team is getting slighted or when they aren't playing well? How do you react?

Have there ever been times during a game when the tension was so great that you said or did something you regretted later?

If you are prone to arguing intensely or harassing officials, the opposing team, or even your own players, it's time to assess the price of taking such an aggressive approach.

Ask yourself: *Is it costing your team? Is it costing you?*

Your reputation amongst peers, officials, and even players will precede you when your team travels or plays a new team. How is that important? If it's negative, or you have a history of losing control, it often sets the wrong tone. It creates greater tension and often a bias against your program. Ultimately, it could cost you the game. Is that fair? Certainly not, but we'll always be a representative of our program and accountable for our actions.

What do your players see? Are you a role model for them? Do they want to be a coach like you some day? Will you be able to ask them to keep their composure in tough situations when they see you can't? The respect you need to lead them is tarnished bit by bit with every incident, and it may be lost forever.

While losing control has the potential to cost you on any given night with your team, what about your career? Remember, it's not just you yelling and screaming. You *are* the school you work for. Being a coach and representing a school is a huge responsibility, one that shouldn't be taken lightly. If you develop a pattern of unruly behavior, the school or organization may have no recourse but to fire you, regardless of your outstanding credentials.

How about your family when they attend your games? What do they see? Can you really justify your actions to them?

For all the issues highlighted above, you need to ask *is your behavior costing you? Could it cost you your team, your job, the people you care about most?*

Let's look at some of the reasons coaches become so upset:

- One of our players is injured on a dangerous play.
- We believe an official missed a call.
- Officials ignore us.
- Our team is not playing well.
- Our team is arguing with each other.
- Officiating doesn't appear to be consistent.
- The opposing coach is yelling at our players and us.
- The game is out of control with respect to safety.

There are more situations we could mention, but I'm sure you've either seen or experienced many. For some coaches, the justification for aggression is to say, "I was protecting my players!" That certainly has merit in situations where the safety of players is concerned but does it help to unleash a profanity-laced tirade that may get you ejected? I don't believe so. In this case, your players need you now more than ever. So, how do we deal with situations where we're at boiling point, ready to explode?

All coaches know the boiling point I'm talking about. Once you break it, there's no turning back. What can you do to help stay calm?

- Walk away and take a deep breath for a moment. Think things through.
- Make your point strongly without abusive language
- Recognize when you are about to go through your boiling point and walk away from the conversation.
- Stay away from making it a personal attack.
- Ask the official what they saw. Plead your case in a professional manner.

- Have a solid assistant who has the power to pull you back or calm you down if needed.

- If the game is totally out of hand with respect to safety, take your team off the field. No game is worth seeing your players get deliberately hurt.

- If possible, wait, and deal with your team issues at practice the next day.

- Ignore anything coming from the opposing bench. You have a team to coach. Let your AD handle that if needed.

Being thrown out of a game will rarely be what's best for your players, your school, and your family. How can you stand up for your players when you're forced to leave the field? There will be games where the discipline to bite your tongue, and not to say what you want to say, is almost impossible but you have to be able to do that. Take a deep breath and ask yourself, "Will my getting thrown out of this game to make a point, help my team or me?"

When the game is over, and you've shown great discipline in an almost impossible situation, and someone says, "Coach, I don't know how you did it. I would have gotten thrown out of that game!" be proud of everything you did for your players, the school, your family and yourself. It's never easy, but it's always the right thing to do.

38

Postgame Interviews... Did I Really Say That?

Have you taken the time to talk with your players about what they say (and how they say it) in interviews? I highly recommend it! Have you given thought to your own interview training? Many coaches and players learn through experience, but that can prove costly with the slip of a word or phrase at an emotional time.

Most colleges and professional teams have a media specialist whose job is to teach players and coaches proper etiquette, inflection, and pronunciation for an interview, along with phrases and situations to avoid. But what about those teams without a budget for a specialist?

There have probably been times when you've read or seen one of your own interviews and asked yourself, "Did I really say that?" After a highly competitive game, especially one you've lost, emotions run high, and you say something you shouldn't have, even if it's true. With that in mind here are some tips to think about before the next reporter sticks a microphone in your face or calls you:

1. **ESCAPE** - Immediately after talking with your team following an emotional game, distance yourself from reporters. Find a place to collect your thoughts before they arrive. If it's a local reporter, set the parameters for the time and place for the interview before the season.

2. **CALM DOWN** - Take a deep breath or two and do your best to relax. Remember your passion has been running high, so give it time to subside.

3. **STAY POSITIVE** - During the interview talk about all the positives you observed. Leave all your excuses out. This is not the time to blast officials or players in a public forum. While you may feel the need to do that, it will never change the outcome, and will appear worse tomorrow when printed or played.

4. **COMPLIMENT THE OTHER TEAM** - Regardless of the outcome or ability of the opposition, always say something positive about them. Goodwill can only help you down the road. If you've ever lost, you know that reading a few kind words the next day from the other coach can really mean something.

5. **FOCUS ON YOUR TEAM** - Talk about your team, regardless of the tactics or actions of the opposition (which you may have disagreed with). There's no need to throw a jab at the other team concerning their ability.

6. **RECOGNIZE NO WIN QUESTIONS** - Questions such as, "XYZ School has been quoted as saying they'll run the score up on you considering what happened last year. What's your reaction to that?" Never answer a question that hasn't been verified or which serves no purpose in helping your team. Reporters are just trying to create the night's hot story.

7. **STAY WITH FACTS, NOT PREDICTIONS** - Keep the interview on track with what your team has accomplished. Avoid predictions, they just become motivation for other teams and add undue pressure to your team.

8. **OUR TEAM** - One phrase that really bothers me is when a player or coach says, "Tonight my team really…" It's OUR TEAM, not *my* team or *your* team. Practice using the phrase and it'll become a habit.

9. **PRACTICE** - The only way to improve at interviews is to practice. Use your smartphone to record a mock interview. Have one of your teammates, another coach, or your spouse ask the questions. Play it back and critique yourself. Think about how others (such as players, parents, and the other team) might perceive your answers from *their perspectives*. You may want to watch clips of coaches you admire giving interviews.

10. **ASSISTANT COACH** - In certain situations, you may be best served by allowing your assistant coach do the interview. It serves two purposes: it gives the assistant experience, and if you're upset (and can't let things go) it prevents outbursts from emerging.

Your interview becomes the voice and image for your team. The program is judged rightly or wrongly from your words, reactions, and emotions. Interviews are more than just something you're required to do before or after a game. They give those who are familiar (and not so familiar) a glimpse of what your program is all about. Embrace the media; they have a job to do just like you. Use them in a positive way to build the image of your program and promote its values.

Be aware that interviews can go viral if you lose control of your emotions and words. Sadly, those words can never be erased, so be prepared for any question that may come your way. Choosing words that will best serve your team going forward is the sensible choice. Read or watch that interview the next day and be proud in knowing that you did the right thing.

39

Over-Coaching... Can You Hear It?

What would you consider 'over-coaching' to be? Most would probably agree that a coach yelling and screaming on the sidelines for the entire game and constantly directing players like robots would qualify.

From another perspective, what if your boss came in every five minutes or so and yelled instructions at you? I'm pretty sure you'd be looking for another job. After all, he or she hired you with confidence, and should trust that you can do the job.

All you have to do is watch a soccer game and see coaches patrolling the sidelines and barking continuously. The fans have come to expect it, and when a coach remains calm, they don't think he or she is doing their job. It's one of the models young coaches see and build their demeanor from. People think that is how a coach should behave. But is it?

Let's face it; there will be times when you have to yell or shout instructions because of the crowd's noise or to make an important point. But all the time? Coaches from their very DNA feel the need to be in control, and there's nothing wrong with that until it becomes an obsession. Can you control your team without being a screamer and yeller? I think so.

How can you look at your demeanor on the sidelines in a different light? Consider the following:

- Often players can't hear what you're yelling.
- If they're paying attention to you, how can they focus on the game?
- Did you prepare the players in practice?
- Do they know when they've made a mistake?
- Will yelling help the players' composure when they need it most?

- How would you feel if your AD yelled at you in front of the fans?

- Do you trust your players? At what point will you trust them?

- Is the yelling for you or your players?

- Is there a better time to correct the problem?

- Does yelling at them really make them tougher?

- Are you making them dependent on everything you say? What are you creating when you're not there?

Is there a way to break the cycle? What steps could you take to start trusting your players' decisions during a game?

- Simply refrain from saying everything that comes to mind, especially in low-pressure moments for the players.

- Work in increments of time. Be silent for a number of minutes, and build up to more time, each game, when possible.

- Make voice notes on your phone of what changes or adjustments need to be made, or talked about, during a timeout or halftime and wait.

- Take a deep breath during a challenging time and give the players a chance to make decisions. Encourage them in a positive tone to stay focused.

- When a mistake is made, keep a calm demeanor. You'll have time to talk to individual players when you take them out, or at halftime.

- Think about *what* you're yelling. Is it something you should have worked on in practice, something totally new, or not even that important?

- Be clear on instructions before the game and when you put a new player in the game.

- Have one of your assistants remind you discreetly when you return to yelling every instruction.

- Remind yourself that being quiet at times is for the benefit and growth of your players.

This will take some practice for coaches who've adopted a yell-all-the-time style and feel the need to continue it. Keep in mind that you can still patrol the sidelines with intensity. This isn't about taking power away from the coach; it's about freeing up your players to make the decisions you want, by being able to do it on their own. By trusting your players, they'll be able to impact games in a positive way, and you'll be happily surprised at some of the great decisions they make on their own.

Watch basketball coach Mike Krzyzewski of Duke during a game. Love him or hate him and his program, Coach K remains seated most of the game. During timeouts, he's as vocal and fiery as any coach you'll see, and if there's any doubt if that style works, just check out the program's success over his career.

Prepare your team the best you can in practice, and give them the power to make tough decisions during the game. It'll pay big dividends in key moments when they can't hear you.

40

What Would You Tell Your Athletic Director?

What type of professional relationship do you have with your Athletic Director? I've had several ADs during my career, and they all treated me with respect, as I did them. I admire the way they do their jobs and marvel at how they juggle all their responsibilities, including attending as many games as possible, paperwork, evaluations, parents, and demanding coaches.

At some levels, such as high school and small colleges, Athletic Directors are a one-man or one-woman show. There just isn't enough funding to give them the support they need. The challenge is to find time to communicate with all the coaches and give them the support they need.

Often Athletic Directors will not spend much time with the coaches they trust and those who are doing a good job with their teams. While this appears to be a good situation for some coaches, I believe it does them a disservice. Coaches need input: positive input or areas of concern.

Many coaches might not necessarily approach their Athletic Directors with some of the issues/statements I've compiled below, but for them to be successful, improve, grow and have the support they need, the following must be addressed:

- **TRAIN ME TO BE A BETTER LEADER** - Most of us are schooled in the X's and O's of our sports. It doesn't mean we stop learning. We seek advantages in these areas every day, but often we neglect our leadership skills. Yes, we use them every day, but are they the best they can be?

- **IF NEEDED, DISCIPLINE ME** - This is an area that most coaches don't like to deal with, especially when it comes to infractions or issues that pertain to us. However, in certain situations, we expect to be disciplined, and when we aren't, it diminishes our respect for the AD and opens the door for us to think it is okay to step over the line.

- **LET ME KNOW WHEN YOU DON'T SEE MY BEST** - I expect my AD to be open and honest with me when they see I'm not giving everything I can for my school and my team. We all need someone to step up and let us know. It doesn't mean we like it, but we understand.

- **EVALUATE MY SEASON IN A STRONG WAY** - For us to grow and improve, we need an unbiased evaluation of our season. We can come up with reasons and excuses for failures, but that view from someone outside our sport is critical.

- **REQUIRE GOAL SETTING AND A PERSONAL GROWTH PLAN** - Coaches need to set goals and establish a growth plan for their program. Without a road map, we will never reach our destination.

- **I NEED YOUR OPINION AND WHAT YOU SEE** - I want my AD to visit my practices frequently. Input on my ability to motivate and challenge my players will assist me in being successful.

- **BE CONSISTENT IN EVERY DECISION YOU MAKE** - Just as we have to be consistent in our decisions with our players, I need my AD to be consistent in coaching decisions with respect to funding, facilities, discipline, etc.

- **BE FAIR TO MY SPORT WITH RESPECT TO FUNDING** - Explain in detail how you arrived at the funding for my sport and my team. Leave nothing hidden or unexplained.

- **ENCOURAGE ME, I NEED IT** - Every coach I know needs encouragement. We thrive off of someone letting us know how much they appreciate the job we're doing.

- **SHOW ME HOW. DON'T BLAME ME. I BLAME MYSELF ENOUGH** - Be clear in what the expectations for my job are. If I mess up, I'm usually the first to realize it. When we meet, let me know how I can correct any situation that arises.

- **MY RESPECT FOR YOU IS BASED ON YOUR ACTIONS, NOT YOUR WORDS** - As my players watch me to see if my actions live up to my words, I will always be watching you. If you say it, mean it.

- **LOOK ME IN THE EYE WHEN YOU HAVE TO LET ME GO** - Don't let me hear it from someone else, or a phone call. Call me in and look me in the eye when it's my time to leave. None of us likes this situation, but it is the professional way to do it.

- **I DON'T NEED ANOTHER FRIEND** - A cozy relationship with an AD is not an ideal situation. While socializing or attending school functions is necessary, remember there may come a day when they have to let you go. I have always had a pleasant relationship with my ADs over the years based on professionalism. Just keep in mind that both of us have a job to do.

I'm not sure how Athletic Directors do it. As coaches, we have the joy and thrill of a player making a fabulous play, or our team winning a big game. That feeling keeps us motivated and longing for more. There are no personal big games for an Athletic Director other than to feel proud of one or more of the school's teams being successful.

It's a job that requires a special person, one who's willing to do anything possible to support the school's programs. One of the most important things they can do is to communicate constantly with their coaches, doing their best to cover all the areas mentioned. Remember, coaches may not vocalize it, but they count on ADs.

A special thank you to all the Athletic Directors and all you do.

41

Becoming A Top Coach...
Are You Ready?

Local and national coaching organizations do a wonderful job of educating coaches. I've certainly benefitted greatly through their dedication to our profession.

In addition to participating in such groups, we spend a lot of time, money and resources immersed in webinars, books, and DVDs developed by successful coaches in order to improve our ability to coach our teams. Many of us attend residential courses on styles of coaching, developing a philosophy, selecting our team, game management and organizing a practice.

We're all looking for that edge, that one idea that will be the key to motivating our players, breaking down a defense, or finding an attacking formation to win a championship.

There are other ways – easily accessed and close to home – to improve our coaching abilities for every practice, every game, and every season but which we often overlook.

At practically no cost, here are nine that will make an immediate impact and benefit your career. The only requirement is that you're strong enough to see your coaching habits through the eyes of others whom you trust.

- **VIDEO -** Have someone videotape practice and your sideline during a game as a teaching tool. We know how valuable it is for a player to see themselves either doing something great, or something that needs to be improved. The same is true of us. At practice, did I do a good job of explaining? Did I paint a picture when they got it right? Would I be motivated by my coaching style? What's my demeanor on the sidelines?

- **ASSISTANT COACH -** Do you have an assistant coach who is brave and willing enough to give you honest feedback on your performance? Remember, if you both agree on everything, one of you isn't necessary! Ask for their assessment every day. On a scale of 1-10, rate today's practice/game? What did you see that you like? What needs improvement? What would you recommend? What about my performance?

- **ATHLETIC DIRECTOR -** Is your Athletic Director strong enough to ask you tough questions? If they don't ask tough questions, go to them and let them know you need to be evaluated and observed more than once or twice a year. After all, you're directly responsible to them. Being asked to justify why we do certain things is good because it makes us question our actions.

- **ANOTHER COACH -** Ask another coach (retired, former, or from another sport) to evaluate your practice and game situations. Take advantage of someone who has walked in your shoes, and whom you trust to be honest in the evaluation. You may not even know you're doing something that needs to be changed. Ask them to be straightforward in their assessment and opinion.

- **DIFFERENT PERSPECTIVE -** Very often someone who is not close to the team and has little experience in coaching can give you a new perspective. Maybe they have experience in running a business and leading people. What they can tell you through observations can be energizing and eye-opening. Trust their opinion about the team's attitude, demeanor, and properly consider any suggestions they offer.

- **PLAYERS -** Trust your players to give you feedback on practice and games. Develop an evaluation with your players that hits all the key points. Teach your players how to evaluate others in a professional way, and use yourself as an example. They stand to benefit the most from your improvement.

- **FORMER PLAYERS -** Invite a former player to evaluate practice or a game. If you're not experiencing the success you had a few years ago, it could be something you aren't stressing that you did before. Former players will pick up on it immediately and let you know.

- **REVISIT CHAMPIONSHIP PLANS -** Take the time to dig out old practice plans, game situations, and more, from those seasons which were so successful. You'll rekindle that passion, and may find a hidden gem that worked so well with a previous team.

- **EVALUATING YOUR PERFORMANCE** - Evaluate your performance after each practice, each game. Do you make notes (positive and negative) about the activity? Why was it successful (or not)? Was it the activity, the players, or you? How can you make it more effective? Was I enthusiastic? Did I over-coach?

Using every available resource is what successful coaches do. They never quit searching for that edge when it comes to improving their leadership skills to lead their team.

Your team is counting on you to be at your best in practice and on game day. Take advantage of the qualified people who, through their expertise and methods, can assist you in becoming a better coach. Never be afraid to find areas which may need improvement. After all, becoming a top coach is what you are searching for,

42

Reflections... How Does Your Team Shine?

Have you wondered how your team is perceived? Are they seen as unique or just a reflection of today's society and values? Do you care? Should you?

It probably isn't one of your main goals, as you begin coaching your new team, but where exactly does that reflection begin? What gives it clarity or murkiness? Is it that simple to evaluate a team on what you see?

I must admit that early in my career, my players and I weren't as polished as we should have been. Our team had some skilled players and some who were more about physicality than finesse. The reflection we projected was a team without much skill, and we weren't respected in the soccer community. That changed over the years as skill levels improved and I gained an understanding of my role as a leader and influencer with my team.

I have great respect for teams that reflect the following qualities, and I always worked to cultivate them in my players:

1. **HUMILITY** - We see a lot of showboating in sporting events, with players pounding their chests with an "It's all about me," attitude. I always tell my players, "When you score or do something terrific, act like you've done it before and move on. You can celebrate later." If you've been on the losing side of the score, you know how the other team feels, especially if you're winning big. Remember, others on our team contributed to making that play possible and show your gratitude to them in a humble way.

2. **SUPPORT** - Show your support and appreciation for your teammates while they play if you're not in the game. While on the field, support and encourage one another every chance you get. As you watch a team, it is obvious if they support each other or if they are just a collection of individuals.

3. **RESPECT** - Always respect decisions made by your teammates, coaches, and officials during the game. I know I'm old school, but using the phrases, "Yes ma'am" and "No ma'am" and "Yes sir" and "No sir," especially to the officials, is a good habit to get into. If you disagree with something, talk to your coach or teammates after the game in a quiet setting. Always respect the game and your opponent.

4. **FOCUS** - Maintain your focus throughout the game, especially during a big win or big loss. Your actions during those times define who you are. Coming out of the game, taking off all your gear, and sulking when things aren't going right, or clowning around with your teammates on the sideline during a big win, is never acceptable.

5. **DETERMINATION** - Work relentlessly, even if it's for a losing cause in a lopsided game. Everyone sees that determination, and it will only help you as the season progresses. I've often heard my players and other coaches and officials on the sidelines talk in glowing terms when they see a player work hard regardless of the score.

We're always in charge of our team. When they show up, how they warm up, how mentally prepared they are, and, ultimately, how they play.

Their demeanor is a reflection of us. If they deviate from acting responsibly, it's our job to bring them back. That's not always easy with influences from TV, social media, friends, and other conflicting messages they might receive from home. Gaining respect from other teams, officials and coaches takes time. While respect may not be one of our primary objectives, establishing self-discipline is because it's a building block of success.

A team on the field, and on the sidelines, is a great indicator of what type of coach they have. It doesn't take long to assess character. That reflection should always be a priority. After all, immature or selfish behavior by players causes ripples that distort the image of a team and a school. That team's reflection will always be you.

43

Asking Tough Questions... of Ourselves

There are a lot of forms available which help us to evaluate our players, and there's inevitably one that our ADs use to evaluate us. But have you ever spent time thinking about what an evaluation form for yourself might look like? Not necessarily for the past season, but one that also covered where your program is today, the direction it is heading, and your coaching performance.

You may have said to yourself during routine evaluations, "I could come up with better questions than that!" Could you be objective in the criteria? Could you be completely honest in your answers?

No one is tougher on us than ourselves when we're passionate, committed, and dedicated to our team. We've all spent nights asking "why" and "how" when our team wasn't successful or was uncharacteristically mistake-prone. While some coaches may not have the resources or experience to generate ideas on how to improve their weaknesses or expand their strengths, who better knows what those weaknesses or strengths are?

Let's look at some questions to consider as we look in the mirror.

- On a scale of 1-10, what is my level of commitment and dedication to our team?

- What did my players learn from me in a loss? A win?

- Am I strong enough to trust my players in key situations?

- Does my program have a philosophy of shared leadership?

- What is my biggest weakness?

- Are my players free to share ideas or suggestions?

- Am I spending adequate time preparing for practice?

- Did I thank my assistants for all their efforts?

- Am I prompt?

- Is my demeanor on the sideline constructive?

- Do I berate a player who makes a mistake?

- What is my level of enthusiasm?

- Did I meet with players who didn't make our team?

- Am I a positive role model on and off the field?

- Did I mention and highlight one or more role players to the media this season?

- Was I gracious in my remarks when asked about our opponent?

- What meaningful roles do my assistants have?

- Do I overuse nonspecific comments such as Good job! Great idea! Unlucky!

- How good am I at communicating with our AD?

- How good am I at delegating responsibilities to my assistants and our team leaders?

- Do I have a system for dealing with challenges outside the game?

- Am I able to hold players accountable consistently?

- How would I rate my character and integrity?

- Am I brief when making a point in a teachable moment?

- Was I humble in a win, gracious in a loss?

- Did I represent our players at state/national award meetings?

- Is my decision making consistent?

- Am I involved in continual coaching education?

- Did I make an effort to visit officials before the game this season?

- What was our level of success this season? How is our success defined?

- What are my plans for our team next year?

- Do I always look in the mirror first in times of crisis?

- What is one incident this year that I wish I'd handled differently?

- From delegating, enthusiasm, character, planning, teaching, trust, communication and game situations, which two are my strongest? Which two need work?

- Did I deflect blame from our players for a loss this season to myself?

- Does my team have a list of expectations?

- What was our biggest team reward this season?

- Was I completely honest with players concerning their roles?

- If necessary, can I talk to my team in a sincere heartfelt manner?

- Did I do my best to thank those who work behind the scenes?

- Am I building a program or just planning season to season?

- Did I meet with parents before the season?

- Did I contact teachers with respect to our players' conduct and responsibilities?

- What was wrong with this season? What was right?

- Am I challenging players to improve at every opportunity?

- Did I involve our players in the community?

- Did I provide leadership classes or team building activities for our team?

- Will I coach this team again next season?

- Do I know the talents our players have outside our game?

- What are my coaching principles?

- Do I only stop play in practice when mistakes are made?

- Did I pitch in and help with fundraising activities?

- How do I deal personally with a loss?

- Would I consider myself a good listener? Why or why not?

It's impossible to have a perfect score on all questions, but it shouldn't deter us from striving to be the best coach we can become. There will be times when we act out of character, perhaps when asked about an incident that may have led to a loss. It happens. Recognizing it, and using it as a learning tool is imperative. The important part is that we, as coaches, come up with our own questions that will allow us to grow and evaluate our performances. As we continue our careers, the questions will continue to pop up. It's our way of checking the GPS to see if we're on the right road.

It's not always about the challenges we face; there are many questions when our season is a success as well. By looking in the mirror, we face our toughest critic, the one who doesn't allow us to relax and always says, "You can do it. You're on the right track. Don't give up!"

Bennion Kearny publishes a lot of books
for the Soccer Coach.

You can see all our soccer books at:
www.BennionKearny.com/Soccer

<< Or click on the QR code to the right >>

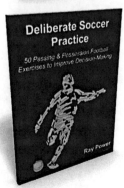

CPSIA information can be obtained at www.ICGtesting.com
Printed in the USA
LVOW10s0243051016

507460LV00016B/304/P